THE PRIVATE INTEREST FOUNDATION OF PANAMA

By Marc M. Harris

HARRIS PUBLISHING, INC.
Panama. Panama

The Private Interest Foundation of Panama

by
Marc M. Harris

ISBN: 9962-5505-1-3

Cover map courtesy of: Old Historic Maps & Prints
www.raremaps.com

PREFACE

P anama may well be the least known and most low profile tax haven in the entire world, unlike other tax havens which are constantly pushed into the financial limelight by those itching to undermine all asset protection systems in the Free World. Wealthy individuals from all over the world open one or more financial entities in Panama just because the scrutiny in the US, as well as in other havens, is becoming too much to stomach. This low profile has given it the perfect smoke-screen reputation for people who are serious about protecting their assets in offshore surroundings.

Panama has many asset protection vehicles to offer its international clientele. One of these is the Private Interest Foundation. As part of Panama's continuous effort to maintain a leading role as one of the predominant offshore tax havens centers of the world, the Legislative Assembly of Panama approved Law No. 25 of 1995, which regulates Foundations of Private Interest, commonly known as Private Interest Foundations. This law regulating Private Interest Foundations has been inspired, and to a large extent modeled after, the law regulating the Family or Mixed Foundations (Stiftung) of the Principality of Liechtenstein, which has for many years been widely used in Europe and in particular Switzerland. Consequently, while there are great simi-larities with the Liechtenstein law, there are a few innovations which make the Panamanian law more modern and more flexible than the Liechtenstein model.

This manual has compiled all the necessary information you will need to know about Panamanian Private Interest Foundations and how they can lead you to a more secure method of protecting your assets offshore in a country in which privacy is not the exception, but the rule!

TABLE OF CONTENTS

PART I
INSIDE
PANAMA

PROFILE

P anama is a country that has been discovered by the financial giants of the world and most people are astounded when they find out that there are more than 140 international banks located in the city limits alone! How many international banks do you have in your city?

Panama also has the most favorable commercial secrecy laws in the world. These ensure a client's privacy when dealing with the top-level firms in the country. While, legal changes in the Caribbean and Europe have caused a loss of banking privacy and because of this, Panama is rapidly becoming the number one offshore financial center of the world. Panama is known as the "Bridge of the Americas" and "Crossroads of the World" and has become the prime location for financial migration between the two continents and the two oceans. Panama has several other interesting attributes that make it the most attractive financial center for Americans.

◆ Panama's currency is the US Dollar, which is circulated freely and without exchange controls on the basis of a 1904 agreement between the United States and Panama.

♦ Panama's time zone is Eastern Standard, ensuring investors of keeping convenient hours to transact business.

♦ Panama has the second largest Free Trade Zone in the world, attracting international executives on a regular basis.

♦ With over 140 international banks, Panama serves as the financial center for all of Latin America and the Caribbean.

♦ In 1925, Panama was the first country in Latin America to enact a trust law.

♦ Panama has a modern airport, excellent telecommunications, and a state of the art financial infrastructure, ensuring individuals and corporations unparalleled services.

ADVANTAGES OF PANAMA

Situated on the isthmus between North and South America, the Republic of Panama covers 29,761 square miles, and is flanked by the Atlantic and Pacific Oceans. The official language is Spanish, but because of the many years of US influence in the cities of Panama and Colon a high percentage of the population also speak English. The economy of Panama is based primarily on private enterprise and depends heavily on the services sector, which is closely geared to international trade and external factors.

Since the time of the Spanish conquerors through the California Gold Rush of 1849 and then the Panama Canal, banking has always played an important role in Panama. In it, some of the largest and best-known banks operating internationally support Panama's bank secrecy laws. The Banking Law and Numbered Account Law contain provisions intended to guarantee banking confidentiality. In fact, these laws forbid banks to disclose details of their clients' transactions to both national and foreign authorities. This secrecy is the major determinant of Panama's obvious success as the most important financial center in Latin America. The United States and Panama also signed a Mutual Legal Assistance Treaty covering money laundering. Nevertheless, the United States failed to persuade Panama to include tax evasion in the treaty because they feared it would prove extremely unfavorable to the offshore banking business.

Other factors have also played a part, including the absence of any currency restrictions, the free circulation of the US dollar as a legal tender, the free international movement of capital, taxation laws typical of so-called "tax havens", and the lack of a central bank in charge of currency issuance. Despite the unusual monetary system, or lack thereof, foreign investors in Panama enjoy the convenience of using a wide variety of currency for business. This is largely due to the international use of the canal and financial sectors, as well as a rapidly expanding tourism industry.

BANKING

Long recognized as a commercial beehive of the Americas since it was a converging point of world steam-ship lanes, Panama had similarly developed into a banking and foreign exchange center. The National Banking Commission and the Governments' wholly owned commercial bank, Banco Nacional de Panama (BNP), administer and supervise Panama's central banking functions. However, no central bank really exists, as the monetary supply is not ruled by any national institution as this process takes place automatically through external factors.

With the closing down of most banks during the 1988 political strife resulting from the Noriega upheaval, a number of major foreign banking offices and branches left the country, but virtually all have returned. Panama's banking system, patterned after the United States banking system, has once again increased to more than 140 commercial banks. Under Panama's revised banking legislation, the banks make sure assets have not evolved from money laundering operations and are required to scrutinize any transaction exceeding $10,000. The National Banking Commission has the authority to inspect the accounting records of a bank, as it may require determining the solvency of banking institutions and compliance with the provisions of Cabinet Decree No. 238. However, the Decree specifically safeguards the confidentiality of the records of deposits and securities belonging to private individuals or companies. The Commission is prohibited to conduct or to order investigations of the private affairs of any bank's client. The information obtained by the Commission may not be revealed to any person or authority except, if it is requested by a court of law or utilized as part of consolidated data for statistical purposes. There are penalties for violation of this precept.

Inspired by the 1970 banking law that guarantees free movement of funds and lower taxes, more than 30 countries have been represented with commercial banks in Panama. Total number of companies registered has soared to more than 285,000.

More than 6,000 Panamanians are employed by the banks, with 85 foreign banks operating in Panama. Net assets of foreign banks grew by $8 billion in the last five years and their level of liquidity is high. Of the 140 banks officially registered, more than 70 provide full domestic and foreign services, 29 are licensed strictly to conduct international operations and the remainders are representative offices. A number of major American banks have opened branches in Panama in order to provide their customers with financing outside of the United States and to facilitate the use of Eurodollar borrowings. Many banks use their Panamanian branches to channel Eurodollars into Central and South American markets, while some of the banks are also active in financing trading. It is important to point out that offshore banking operations are exempt from Panamanian income tax.

In a world moving toward greater globalization, Panama's flexibility in dealing and experiencing a multitude of financial factors including banking, taxes and trade, establish it as a prime location in which to conduct local as well as global business.

TAXATION LAW

Panama is a tax haven and is, as a result, especially attractive to foreign investors. Panamanian tax law is rooted on the territorial principle. As for income tax, the territorial principle applies so that income generated outside of the country is tax-exempt, although the individual or corporation generating the income is domiciled in Panama. There are some certain earnings that are exempt from income tax because they are considered to be of foreign source, and others that, though they arise from a Panamanian income source, are exempt from income tax in Panama. *(See Appendix E)*

The normal corporate tax rate on local Panamanian source income starts at 39% on income up to $100,000 and graduates to 42% on income over $500,000. Corporate dividends and earnings of branches of foreign corporations are subject to a 10% withholding tax if they conduct local Panamanian business. Interest paid or credited to the account of a foreign lender by a local Panamanian enterprise is subject to a 6% withholding tax. Interest on bonds, notes and other registered securities is taxed a flat 5% withholding tax unless traded on a registered exchange in Panama or paid by a Panamanian company with no local Panamanian operations. Income earned within Panama, including the proceeds of sales made within the country, is subject to Panamanian tax.

Historically, one of the major factors responsible for the 35,000 holding companies and tax sanctuary operations established in Panama by foreign businesspersons has been the relative tax freedom. Panama does not assess any income tax on income produced from sources outside the country, including the proceeds of sales made outside of Panama. This territorial method of taxation is only one of the many advantages of incorporating in Panama.

POLITICAL AND ECONOMIC STABILITY

With the Noriega problem now solved, the Government of Panama again welcomes foreign investment and holding companies. In the past, it has gone out of its way to assist overseas investors, in addition to pointing out that foreign executives should receive the same treatment as Panamanians. Since 1990, Panama has passed a series of major Constitutional reforms designed to strengthen the democratic process. These included the abolition of the Armed Forces, one of the most significant changes in Panama's political history.

The economy in this country of 2,400,000 persons has remained far stronger than most observers had predicted. Tourism continues to recover, with more than 400,000 visitors annually in 1996, a rise of 10.5 percent, and generating more than $300 million of income. Inflation is only 2.3%, one of the lowest in all of Latin America.

Gross national product is growing by 2.5% annually while new employment remains at 5%. According to official sources, real GDP grew to $6,354.4 million in 1996, an improvement relative to the prior year rate of 1.8 percent. The unemployment rate has dropped from 31 to 13.9 percent.

Tourism earnings rose 10.5 percent to $338.9 million. In an effort to attract foreign investors in tourism, the Government has outlined a $700 million development plan for investment over the next five years to improve resort facilities on the Atlantic and Pacific coasts.

Total trade passing through the Colon Free Zone now exceeds that reached during the Noriega regime, traffic has recovered and is now close to $10.2 billion. The Colon Free Zone, which accounts for 5% of gross domestic product, enjoys steady growth while Panama Canal traffic, representing 10% of GDP, is climbing at a moderate 2%. To make up for the reduced expansion in Canal traffic, tolls have been increased by a two-step method implemented during fiscal years 1997 and 1998. The first rate increase is of 8.2 percent and took effect on January 1, 1997. The second was implemented on January 1, 1998, with an increase of 7.5 percent.

Exports have risen steadily since 1988, reaching $600 million, while imports have skyrocketed to $2.5 billion, registering a trade deficit of $1.9 billion. Imports arrive chiefly from the United States, Japan and Taiwan, while two-thirds of the re-exports go to the Caribbean and Latin America, especially the Netherlands Antilles, Colombia, Ecuador and Venezuela.

INVESTMENT FACTORS

A positive attitude toward free enterprise, together with the fact that the US dollar is legal tender in Panama, has led to an increase in foreign investments. Moreover, the development of institutions and instruments to regulate business activities in Panama has been consistent with its trade-and-services-oriented economy, which is closely connected to the international market and geared to using Panama's geographic position. Consequently, the aim of the legal and institutional framework is to offer many facilities, incentives for the development of international commercial, and service activities in Panama. There are very few requirements regarding the nationality of investors and no restrictions on converting currencies or transferring funds. Consequently, there are very few limitations or restrictive practices on foreign investment, especially for international business operations based in Panama. One of the few exceptions is retail trade, which is reserved for Panamanian nationals.

To attract foreign investment into Panama, the government has developed the necessary institutional and infrastructure facilities, efficient public administrative machinery, extremely favorable and flexible policy guidelines, and attractive fiscal and non-fiscal incentives.

Historically, the policies of the Panamanian government toward foreign investment have been so open that there has never been any need for a formal statement of policy on this subject. Legislation hardly establishes any differences in treatment between nationals and foreigners. Similarly, all foreign investors, regardless of their country origin, are treated equally.

In short, Panama offers the foreign investor a whole gamut of relevant advantages. *(See Appendix D)*

TYPE OF BUSINESS ENTITIES

Panama's legal system is based on civil law, as opposed to common law. Nonetheless, because of its traditional close US business ties,

Panama in 1927 adopted a Corporation Code, which is similar to the old Delaware Corporation Statute.

In addition to the corporation (sociedad anonima), Panama has several types of modern business entities: the single limited partnership, joint stock association, general partnership and limited liability partnership.

The Panamanian entity that has captured the attention of many investors is the Private Interest Foundation, which is very similar to the Liechtenstein Anstalt ("Establishment"), but which can be formed for substantially less cost. Panama enacted in 1995, a law to govern the establishment of this entity, and it presents a serious alternative to standard offshore trusts and corporations. Panamanian Foundations of Private Interest represent a practical legal tool helpful for careful and prudent family or estate planning or for asset protection and privacy purposes.

For years now, Panama has been dedicated in trying to balance itself as a country in order to receive the Canal from the United States, in the best shape possible. The government is making efforts to modernize the economy for the year 2000 by restructuring its foreign commercial debt, completing negotiations to join the World Trade Organization, privatizing government-owned companies, passing legislation to improve the level of economic efficiency, by facilitating its incorporation into the world economy.

PART II
THE PRIVATE
INTEREST
FOUNDATION IN THE
REPUBLIC OF PANAMA

GENERAL INTRODUCTION

The Private Interest Foundation in Panama, hereafter will be called the Panamanian Foundation*See*, is a complex entity and is con sidered a fascinating topic for legal deliberation because of its reflection to the Liechtenstein Family Foundation (Stiftung), which itself is a hybrid of the Anglo-Saxon trust. For lawyers it establishes a true defense scheme of the hereditary assets of the client and his family, while for the administrator or trustee it is the true management model and functional administration tool.

The Panamanian Foundation is basically a donation whose purpose is the creation of a legal entity, which serves to manage and administer individual or non-individual assets assigned to that institution by the Founder. The donation seeks the creation of an ideal administrator or trustee, in this case the Foundation Council, who strives to achieve the goals and objectives sought by the Founder. The Panamanian Foundation is a legal entity that connects two operations: a donation plus a trust with a legal nature due to its registration in Panama's Public Registry.

Fiscal law takes care of the private founding status because of its flexible character, which corresponds as an asset protection instrument, of goods, capital or other valuable intangibles that by being organized under this type of law receives a fiscal treatment of unique character. Family law absorbs it too, because of the terminology used in the laws of Liechtenstein that speaks of family foundations or Stiftung, which translates as Private Interest Foundations in the Panamanian jurisdiction.

Other worthy elements of this entity are that the Panamanian Foundation is unquestionably a complement to the list of other asset protection or hereditary vehicles of the Panamanian civil ordinance. It is a legal entity that is situated between a will and a corporation, but with its own individuality which gives it an autonomous character founded in legal grounds and with the objective of safekeeping the assets given or assigned for managing by its Founder.

An important point to mention is that Panamanian Foundations have no legal relations with other types of foundations. Although the specific law on Panamanian Foundations does not define what it is intended by its meaning, it does exclude, to avoid confusions, assimilation or ambiguity, all judicial business based on the foundation without a lucrative end or purpose (*Civil Code Title 2, Book 1*). The public foundations in Civil Law are those without gains and originated from ideologies in politics, society and religion. Not so in a Panamanian Foundations, which radically narrows it down to only the conservation and protection of an incorporated estate in the foundation for the administration by virtue and trust of the Founder. The regular foundations have a more political and ideological interest while the Panamanian Foundation has an inheritance and privacy guarantee. **The two entities should not be confused.** The Panamanian Foundation also includes the protection and reorganization and planning of local and international estate taxation, as well as individual and corporate tax, as its goal.

The reason for which a person or persons should contemplate creating a hereditary vehicle is defined by the need of transferring an estate, which presumes that whomever frees assets in favor of a beneficiary has the final word in creating a legal entity of this sort. This liberalization of funds is commonly made through a simple procedure or via testate proceedings designating an executor.

In the case of a Panamanian Foundation, this transferring of assets is totally different from an ideological foundation based on political, societal or religious beliefs and without lucrative gain. It does take the same mannerisms of transmitting the assets but with the direct end of, not just transferring, but conserving and protecting assets.

The law ends short of including that any person or persons with a readily available and justifiable estate can establish or incorporate a foundation entity. The above omission in the law radiates from the absence of a Statement of Intent, which gives the origin and cause for installing the particular foundation. The excess flexibility in which the foundation or the Founder or third persons are referred to can obscure the qualification of the said Founder and in the same instance, confuse it with a foundation without lucrative ends, which would be a grave error. With this in mind, it is of utmost importance to establish the two greatest parameters of transparency that will permit us to distinguish the functions of a Panamanian Foundation in respect to a foundation without any lucrative gain, pictured in the Civil Code:

The foundation limits itself to mere acts of conservation of the estate through the handling of the corporate and merging assets.

The first article of this law notes who can form a Panamanian Foundation, as long as it is a moral and natural person requiring the incorporation of their estate which make up the central point of the regulations of this legal entity. Without consent, a foundation, which is the primary gravitational center of accepting corporate and incorporated assets, cannot be established.

The patrimonial or hereditary concept dissociates itself from the concept of an association without lucrative gains, because the associations without lucrative gains have as an objective only the ideological-societal, political and philosophical conception that is not the point here; the Panamanian Foundation concept is totally hereditary. This hereditary concept branches out into keeping accounts and administering the estate which is a passive act combined with the active execution of deciding how to increment or manage the conservation of those assets assigned to the foundation. The administration is simply the hereditary registry, existing for the benefit of the estate, meanwhile, the Foundation Council or a similar entity, is the dynamic and directional professional who carry out said directive to optimize the rentability, productivity and purpose of the estate while investing for the same.

Article 3 of the law examines and refers to the occasional exercises of commerce and states that the Panamanian Foundation can follow and effect acts of commerce when these acts relate to optimizing the value or assets of the foundation and the purpose for why it was established. For example, the sale of a hotel, which is property of the foundation in question, is a perfectly legal and proper activity for the foundation to undertake. However, the foundation cannot operate as a buyer or seller of hotels, because that would then be a strict commercial activity.

The foundation being of incorporated assets, stocks, bonds, and other valuables, can also invest in the stock exchanges or through brokerage firms which can give them a better growth on their assets. This establishes the possibility of a consistent and intelligent way of investing in a financial fashion and at the same time protecting the net worth of the foundation.

Law 25 of June 12, 1995 creates the Panamanian Foundation. As was stated previously, the Panamanian Foundation is no more than a reflection or symmetry of the Liechtenstein Family Foundations, which had their origins in the beginning of the century. The origin of the foundation answers a need of the international tax planners in complementing the Anglo-Saxon Trust figure, as well as reinforcing the services of the corporations or stock companies with bearer shares which are the two key instruments within the asset protection services industry. The foundation constitutes a legal figure which strengthens the wealth management services and, at the same time, the asset protection services and private investments protection services.

The foundation encompasses all the principal elements of the foundation law of February 19, 1926 of Liechtenstein, as well as other significant changes that transform it into a more modern vehicle. Indeed, it is possible that the Panamanian Foundation will soon surpass the Anstalt as the entity-of-choice for sophisticated offshore practitioners.

OBJECT OF THE FOUNDATION

The foundation is defined as an entity or a moral person endowed with an estate whose cause is mere benevolence and that at the same time it is a legal person who has the capacity to make contracts and enter obligations. The purposes of the Panamanian Foundation, are hereditary conservation purposes, that is to say, the handling of such investments or assets transmitted or assigned to the foundation. The same must solely carry out acts of preservation of the estate by increasing it or distributing it based on the mandates stated in the Articles of Foundation and the expressed volition of the founding member.

The foundation cannot devote itself to commercial transaction acts only exceptionally, and consequently it cannot carry out commercial transactions nor are the bankruptcy laws but the common dissolution laws applicable to the same.

TYPES OF PRIVATE INTEREST FOUNDATIONS

Covering the types of foundations is not easy task in view of the grammatical way in which the wording of the foundation was treated in the laws. Corporations are much easier because of their explicit text, which permit a more exact interpretation of the kinds of corporations in the subject. In classifying foundations, it can either be irrevocable or revocable depending on the parameters; on the other hand, it can be established based on the principles of mortis-causa. The following will attempt to explain the different types of Private Interest Foundations:

a) Mortis-causa Foundation: In this case, which can be previewed in Article 4 shows the conditional foundation at the death of the Founder. Article 4 anticipates this foundation, not only as an avenue of private donations, but also for the irrevocable creation of this legal entity. (See Part IV, which includes the complete translation of Law No. 25 of June 12 of 1995, and more specifically Articles 13 and 14)

This norm grows from the ambiguity that a foundation is a one-sided transferable act in a donation that is effective in life if it is established as a testament and could conflict upon the laws of public order of donations in wills. However, the only type of foundation that logically should prevail is the mortis-causa foundation established by a will. The first paragraph of Article 4 begins with the rules of the direction of public order and the norm of wills. It is understood that in fiduciary matters the Founder of a trust creates a trust testament under such autonomous rules and with corresponding formalities. Although, in the rules of the foundation there can be incorporated in it a clause destined to establish a regime of will distribution. Moreover, the correct classification should be a revocable or irrevocable foundation, because it is a distinct function from the trust. This last one has the right of transferring private property; the other has as an objective, for instance, the conservation of the assets and not necessarily the transferring.

b) Irrevocable Foundation: in essence the foundation is presumed irrevocable save the contrary assumptions in the law. Article 12 of the Panamanian Foundation indicates that for a foundation to be revocable it shall be stated in the Foundation Charter.

The irrevocability pretends to give a steadfast explanation and would be in the business of law that the voluntary and truthful examination to reinforce the rules that no one can go against their own acts. It is to say that it deals with the determined decision and not of manipulation or simulation that permits to justly escape a critical and effective law to govern the assets or legal relations in the personal statute of the Founder and the legal entity created.

c) Revocable Foundation: the foundation is revocable when it has been established in the Foundation Charter. Meaning that, in highlighting the autonomy of the Founder for legal causes foreseen in the donation and when there are no inscription in the Public Registry as it expresses in Article 12 of Law No. 25 of June 12, 1995. By will of the Founder, he or she may reserve the right of establishing a stay of the foundation, which at the moment of establishing the determined circumstance or at the end of the term can be retroactivated. This reservation can be predetermined by the Founder and can therefore retroactivate the foundation and incorporate again in the personal statute of the Founder, or in a legal entity different or a legal person different of who was before.

In causes foreordained in the donation, the legal nature of the foundation is based on the donation. This legal instrument obeys its clauses unconstrained, and also could amend itself in case of ingratitude, attempting against the life of the Founder, or whatever preset rules justly stated in the Civil Code that regulates the clauses of revocation of the donation. This is another side of the foundation not registered that is solidified by the revocable foundation by means of a fixed agreement written in presence of a notary but inscribed in the Public Registry. This type of private interest foundation clashes with the values of legal privacy, because it can produce negative effects between the parties, but it cannot be brought up with a third party if the laws of common rights are applied. This kind of foundation explains the character of confidentiality and severity that is preset to justly give the mutation of private property. It can be revoked in 24 hours and activated in 24 hours. This type of foundation operates perfectly when linked to a Foundation Council which professionally respects and administrates the assets in this said legal vehicle.

Finally, nothing impedes the Foundation inscribed in the Public Registry to be revocable; it all depends on the wants and needs of the Founder.

PRIVATE FOUNDATIONS

The Private Foundation under Panamanian law is not related to the foundations that are set up for charity or other civic-minded purposes.

It does not follow the law of those traditional foundations, and at the same time, is not used for profit-oriented reasons either.

The Liechtenstein Family Foundations that are applied widely in Europe inspired the Panamanian foundation. The parallels between the two are extensive; however, the Panamanian foundation was set up with the idea of being more flexible than its Liechtenstein counterpart and less distinctive in areas of the law which separates foundations with regards to legal heirs. While the Liechtenstein foundation disassociates the Family Foundation and the Mixed Foundation, in which the latter can include other heirs not in the immediate family, the Panamanian foundation brings them together in an open-minded way, creating a more modern foundation law.

The Panamanian foundation, as stated above, does not allow its use for profit-oriented matters, but it does approve certain business dealings aimed to achieve the goals and objectives of the foundation, as long as these do not become common practice. The foundation can be executed during the life of the author of the foundation, otherwise known as the Founder, or after his/her death. In each instance, the regulations concerning private foundations will be identical. The creation of a Panamanian foundation begins when the interesting parties' draft the foundation charter, signed by the Founder or Founders, and the same is verified by a notary public. All Private Interest Foundations of the Republic of Panama need to have a Resident Agent to countersign the Foundation Charter before its inscription in the Public Registry and to represent the foundation in Panama. The Resident Agent has to be a Panamanian lawyer or a Panamanian law firm. After the documents and the Founder's signature are authorized by the notary public, the next step would be to register the documents at the Public Registry under a section named, "Section of Private Foundations".

After the registry is completed, the Panamanian foundation becomes a legal entity, and the Founder or other contributors may initiate the transfer of assets to the foundation. Its legal character gives the foundation this right, in addition to, setting up agreements and being able to participate in all business and legal proceedings in accordance with the laws of the Republic of Panama. As a legal entity, the Panamanian foundation shall also abide by the Executive Decree No. 468 of 1994, which attempts to avoid the misuse of the foundation vehicle by potential criminals dealing in drugs or using the instrument as a money laundering scheme.

Private foundations are irrevocable, except when the foundation charter has not been registered at the Public Registry in The Republic of Panama, when the foundation charter affirms otherwise or when any causes of revocation applicable to donations has transpired. Another mandate, which is extremely crucial to Panamanian foundations, is the secrecy factor. Any person, or persons, or legal bodies having to do with all matters involving the foundation, shall maintain utmost secrecy and confidentiality. If a violation of the above occurs, the individual or parties responsible shall be fined $50,000 and could serve a term of up to six months in prison. However the penalties shall be not be brought about if the individual or parties are questioned by the proper Panamanian authorities in regards to criminal activity, such as drug trafficking or money laundering.

Private foundations will pay registration fees and annual taxes of equal value to those in place for a Panamanian corporation at the present time. The procedures and form of payment for any other fees, including late charges or non-payment will also be equal to those being paid in Panamanian corporations.

The domicile of the foundation can be in any place of the world. Due to matters of fiscal interest, it is recommended that the domicile be in the Republic of Panama, although the foundation will be able to carry out its activities abroad. Foundations established in other jurisdictions may become subject to the accordance of this law, if they follow the conditions regulating this transition.

Foundations established in other jurisdictions, which decide to continue as Panamanian foundations, shall submit a document, called the certificate of continuation, indicating its interest in carrying on as such. The certificate of continuation shall be issued by the corresponding body of the foundation, most likely the Foundation Council and shall contain the following:

1. Name and date of constitution of the foundation.

2. Registration, or in some cases termed "deposit", of the vehicle at the initial jurisdiction registry.

3. Disclosure of its petition in becoming a foundation under Panamanian law.

The foreign foundation petitioning continuation shall follow the minimum requirements that are imperative for a Panamanian foundation to be created. These are stated in Article 5 of the present law.

The certificate of continuation and the requirements established above, shall be affixed to the following documentation:

1. Copy of the original act of constitution of the foundation and any amendments created afterwards.

2. A power of attorney ceding legal freedoms to a Panamanian attorney to carry out all the necessary arrangements for the execution of the foundation's continuation as a Panamanian entity.

All documentation presented shall be formalized and registered in Panama's Public Registry for it to legally become a Panamanian foundation.

When a decides to continue its legal existence as a Panamanian foundation, its rights or obligations and any legal proceedings occurring during the change shall not be influenced by the change in jurisdiction.

A Panamanian foundation shall also have the legal right to shift its jurisdiction to a foreign country, if so stated by the foundation charter or its regulations. If the above scenario is considered, then the foreign jurisdiction in which the Panamanian foundation wants to move to, shall need to have in its own laws the acceptance of migration by a Panamanian foundation.

If any conflict arises involving a Panamanian foundation, which this law does not have a solution for, then it shall be resolved by summary proceedings. The Foundation Charter (See The Foundation Charter, pg. #) or its regulations may provide a clause stating, resolution by arbitration, in conflicts arising in connection with the foundation. If and when, no clause has been stated, the conflict shall be handled by the Panamanian Judicial System.

The foundation shall be dissolved for any of the following reasons:

1. On the termination date stipulated in the foundation charter.

2. When the foundation goals and objectives have been met or if their accomplishment becomes impossible.

3. If it becomes insolvent cannot meet payments or is legally declared bankrupt.

4. If the assets become nil.

5. On its revocation.

For any other reason stipulated in the foundation charter or in the present law.

In essence, the Panamanian Foundation is a complementary element of an international asset protection structure and a management tool. It has no owner but beneficiaries, has not shares but is developed through a regulation. The regulation can be prepared by the founding member himself or beneficiary pursuant to the law. Moreover, the succession laws are not opposable, and much less the tax laws concerning the activities that this entity can carry out.

The following advantages are at the heart of the Private Interest Foundation of Panama:

Patrimonial: It creates a separate and autonomous estate from the assets of the Founder.

Judicial: Its assets are unseizable and unencumberable.

Fiscal: It has a fiscal advantage due to its offshore nature on the one hand, and on the other, the family nature for which this institution was created.

Succession: Its assets cannot be attacked by the Founder's heirs because through its statutes its main purpose is preserved, which is the protection of the goods and assets of the Founder.

International: It produces the advantage of being able to change domiciles or nationality or registry or jurisdiction through the statutes regulating the international life of the foundation.

Arbitration: It offers more appropriate ways of dealing with international conflicts by allowing arbitration clauses to regulate, instead of leaving it to ordinary judicial proceedings.

PART III
MAIN
COMPONENTS OF
PANAMANIAN
FOUNDATIONS

THE FOUNDER

The Founder of the private foundation in the Republic of Panama is the person or persons who create the foundation for a non-business purpose. This individual or group of people can be either a common person(s) or a legal entity(ies). Anyone of legal age and exercising free will can create a Panamanian foundation, as long as they follow the procedures stated in the law.

When creating a Panamanian foundation, the Founder is required to furnish the foundation with a specific amount of money. The initial amount is USD$10,000, although this amount does not have to be deposited right away. Either the Founder or third parties wanting to contribute assets to the foundation can in the future increase this initial amount. The Founder, or other parties cited in the Foundation Charter, shall authorize the transfer of assets to the foundation. The assets in the foundation shall also be legally handled as totally separate from those of the Founder's.

The Founder has the right to assign powers to himself or others through the Foundation Charter. One of these powers may consist of adding or removing members of the Foundation Council, which is the supervisory party of the foundation. (See Foundation Council). The foundation charter or its regulations may stipulate the need for the

Foundation Council to obtain its powers through the consent of another duly authorized body appointed by the Founder.

The Founder also has the right to cancel the foundation, even if stated to be effective only after his death. If the Founder states his/her wishes to execute the foundation after their death, the extra formalities that are required in the Civil Code concerning wills shall not be applied and all assets shall be handled as if the foundation was in existence prior to the date of implementation. This eliminates the bothersome act of having to create both, a foundation and a will. Any "forced heirship" laws in the Founder's domicile shall not affect in any way the validity of the foundation and shall not alter the goals that have been set up in the foundation charter or its regulations.

THE FOUNDATION CHARTER

The private foundation in the Republic of Panama has as its most important document, the Foundation Charter. The Foundation Charter contains, among other provisions, specific regulations that are created by the Founder and control all aspects of the foundation. The Foundation Charter shall be registered at Panama's Public Registry, which will render it as a legal entity, without the need of any other legal consent. This will in fact be the foundation's only publicity of existence.

The Foundation Charter is required to include the following elements:

1. Name of the foundation.

2. An initial amount of money.

3. A list of all members of the Foundation Council.

4. Domicile of the foundation.

5. Name and domicile of the chosen agent in the Republic of Panama.

6. The foundation's goals and objectives.

7. The process in which the beneficiaries will be chosen.

8. A decree stating permission to make changes in the Foundation Charter, if necessary.

9. The lifetime of the foundation.

10. A procedure for liquidating the assets and the destination of the same.

It is also stated that the Founder may specify other conditions if he so desires.

When naming the foundation in #1, the Founder shall designate a name that is unlike any other foundation already in existence in the Republic of Panama. To differentiate this, the word "foundation" will be added after the name the Founder has chosen. The amount of money stipulated in #2 shall not be less than USD$10,000 and can be deposited in any currency. The Founder can either be included or excluded in the member list in #3. The agent in charge of handling the affairs of the foundation in #5, shall also sign the Foundation Charter before its registration in the Public Registry. The Founder can either be included or excluded in the beneficiaries in #7.

After creating the Foundation Charter, this document shall be taken to a notary public in the Republic of Panama and protocolized to assure that all regulations needed for the registration of this instrument have been followed. In case the Foundation Charter has been written in any language other than Spanish, the document shall be translated by a certified public translator and notarized for its registration in the Public Registry.

Changes can be made to the foundation, but these shall only be executed by those authorized in the Foundation Charter or its regulations. If this happens, the amendments shall be dated and signed by those empowered to do so, and protocolized by a notary public.

The Foundation Charter shall also agree for the Founder to specify an authoritative body, which can be a Protector, an Auditing Company or a Custodian, to act as the supervising entity of the powers granted to the Foundation Council (See Foundation Council). This supervisory body shall consist of natural or legal persons, whose powers shall be drafted in the Foundation Charter or its regulations and shall consist of the following:

1. To ensure that the Foundation Council is working toward and for the goals of the foundation.

2. To obligate the Foundation Council in providing its administrative dealings.

3. To alter the goals or responsibilities of the foundation when these become impossible to carry out.

4. To assign new members to the Foundation Council, if they have been removed or when their term has expired.

5. To assign new members to the Foundation Council, if any existing members are absent or are temporarily unable to hold office.

6. To increase or reduce the number of members in the Foundation Council.

7. To approve the accounts rendered by the Foundation Council in their workings toward the objectives of the foundation.

8. To act as caretakers of the foundation and oversee that all rules and regulations in the Foundation Charter are being followed.

9. To add or remove beneficiaries of the foundation in accordance to the rules and regulations stipulated in the Foundation Charter and its regulations.

The Foundation Charter or its regulations may also assign other powers to the authoritative body supervising the Foundation Council.

The Foundation Charter or its regulations can also specify the circumstances in which a member of the Foundation Council shall be removed, and the appropriate method for this action. If the Foundation Charter or its regulations do not specify the above, members of the Foundation Council shall be removed by judicial proceedings under the following circumstances:

◆ When there is a conflict of interest between a member and the Founder or his/her beneficiaries.

◆ When a member administers the foundation in a manner not suitable toward its goals.

◆ When a member is convicted of a crime related to private property or public faith. The member can also be suspended from his duties in the Foundation Council while the legal proceedings against him are in effect.

◆ When a member is incapacitated or is somehow unable to continue his duties toward the goals of the foundation.

◆ When a member is insolvent or has filed for bankruptcy.

The Foundation Charter or its regulations may provide a clause stating, resolution by arbitration, in conflicts arising in connection with the foundation.

The duration of the foundation will be established in the Foundation Charter, which can be perpetual.

THE FOUNDATION BY-LAWS

As stated previously, the Foundation by-laws are a parallel and complementary document to the Foundation Charter. These by-laws do not require their inscription in the Public Registry, which guarantees privacy and confidentiality to the beneficiaries and to the way in which the assets of the foundation are distributed. The by-laws include precise instructions about the particular decisions of the Founder.

It is in the by-laws of the foundation where the beneficiaries of the patrimony are named and where any other important information for the Founder or the purposes of the foundation is included, which according to the law is not necessary to be included in the Foundation Charter.

The by-laws of the foundation can be amended according to the needs that arise from time to time.

THE FOUNDATION COUNCIL

The Foundation Council is the supervisory body of the foundation. Its purpose is to carry out the objectives of the foundation and if otherwise stated in the foundation charter, will have the following duties:

1. To administer the assets of the foundation.

2. To handle all business arrangements in accordance to the goals of the foundations and to include in these dealings all suitable conditions convenient to the purposes of the foundation.

In accordance to the specifics in the foundation charter or its regulations, the Foundation Council will have the responsibility of informing the beneficiaries of the foundation the economic situation of the foundation.

In accordance to the specifics in the foundation charter or its regulations, the Foundation Council will have the responsibility of delivering the assets to the beneficiaries that are intended for them.

The Foundation Council shall have responsibility to perform all necessary legal acts that are required for the foundation.

If the last requirement is observed and approved by other authorized bodies, the Foundation Council shall not be held legally accountable for any act or loss of assets pertaining to the foundation.

The Foundation Council will be established in the Foundation Charter where its authoritative powers and responsibilities will be drafted. It shall not be less than three members, except in the case where the Foundation Council is a legal entity, an example would be a corporation or a law firm. The name and domicile of the members of the Foundation Council is of public knowledge and it is not required that the members be Panamanians.

The Foundation Council shall furnish the beneficiaries and if applicable, to the supervisory entity, all accounts of its administrative work, unless the foundation charter or its regulations state otherwise. If there is no provision regarding the above, then the Foundation Council shall render accounts annually. If the rendered accounts are not objected to by the time specified in the foundation charter or its regulations, the accounts shall be assumed approved by the beneficiaries or supervisory entity.

If the foundation charter or its regulations does not specify a time limit for approval, then 90 days from when the accounts were received, shall be the time limit in which the accounts shall be assumed approved. The accounts rendered by the Foundation Council must specify the 90-day requirement for approval in their report. If these 90 days elapse or upon approval of the Foundation Councils report, the members of the Foundation Council will not be held liable for their administration, unless they fail to act towards the goals of the foundation. However, the approval by the overseer of the accounts does not exonerate the Foundation Council, the beneficiaries or others linked to the foundation, of any illegal action or fraud committed through the administrative dealings of the foundation.

If the foundation charter or its regulations do not specify the why and how's of removing a member of the Foundation Council, then members can be removed by judicial proceedings if the following causes can be applied:

1. When there is a conflict of interest between a member and the Founder or his/her beneficiaries.

2. When a member administers the foundation in a manner not suitable toward its goals.

3. When a member is convicted of a crime related to private property or public faith. The member can also be suspended from his duties in the Foundation Council while the legal proceedings against him are in effect.

4. When a member is incapacitated or is somehow unable to continue his duties toward the goals of the foundation.

5. When a member is insolvent or has filed for bankruptcy.

The Founder or his/her beneficiaries may ask for the judicial removal of one or more members of the Foundation Council. If the beneficiaries are incapacitated in some form or fashion or are legally minors, then the legal guardian of these individuals may represent them. If the judicial removal of a member or members take place, then a new member may be appointed which qualifies to administer the assets of the foundation in accordance with the purposes established by the Founder.

The foundation charter or its regulations may stipulate the need for the Foundation Council to obtain its powers through the consent of another duly authorized body appointed by the Founder. The supervisory bodies shall consist of natural or legal persons and their powers shall be established in the foundation charter or its regulations and may include, among others, the following:

1. To ensure that the Foundation Council is working toward and for the goals of the foundation.

2. To obligate the Foundation Council in providing its administrative dealings.

3. To alter the goals or responsibilities of the foundation when these become impossible to carry out.

4. To assign new members to the Foundation Council, if they have been removed or when their term has expired.

5. To assign new members to the Foundation Council if any existing members are absent or are temporarily unable to hold office.

6. To increase or reduce the number of members in the Foundation Council.

7. To approve the accounts rendered by the Foundation Council in their workings toward the objectives of the foundation.

8. To act as caretakers of the foundation and oversee that all rules and regulations in the foundation charter are being followed.

9. To add or remove beneficiaries of the foundation in accordance to the rules and regulations stipulated in the foundation charter and its regulations.

THE FOUNDATION'S ASSETS

Once the foundation has been established by the Founder and registered in the Public Registry it has legal character. This gives it the right to own a variety of assets, set up agreements with other parties and be able to participate in all business and legal proceedings in accordance with the laws of the Republic of Panama. The Founder or other contributors may then deposit assets into the foundation. An initial amount is stated in the foundation charter to be USD$10,000, and it is not necessary for the assets to be transferred at the moment the Foundation is constituted. This allows the valid formation of the Foundation under this temporary arrangement and that in the immediate future it will be capitalized in its entirety. This patrimony can derive from any legitimate business and in which any kind of asset, existing or future, can be transferred to it.

The Founder or others obliged to contribute assets shall also be authorized to transfer assets to the foundation. These assets shall be legally handled as totally separate from the Founder's estate, and may not be subject to any seizures or deemed touchable for any legal reason, except in the case where an injurious action was committed in pursuance of the foundation's goals or of the beneficiaries of the foundation. The transfer of assets is also considered irrevocable, except when otherwise mentioned at the moment of transfer. All transfers of assets should be executed by public or private document, except those which are immovable for example real estate, in which case all of the formalities applied to these kind of transfers shall be heeded.

If the foundation was set up to be effective after the death of the Founder, the assets will be handled as if the foundation was in existence prior to the date of implementation. The heirs of the Founders will have no right after the death of the Founder to annul the foundation or the transfer of assets, even if it has not yet been registered in the Public Registry. In accordance to the specifics in the foundation charter or its regulations, the Foundation Council will have the responsibility of delivering the assets to the beneficiaries that are intended for them.

The creditors of the Founder shall have the right to challenge the transfer of assets or contributions made to the foundation, if the transfer is considered an act of fraud toward the creditors. The above rights will be executable for three years, starting on the date of transfer of the assets to the foundation. If the three years transpire, the right of the creditors to redeem fraudulent assets expires.

The acts which establish, amend, or terminate the foundation, as well as transfer, transmit or encumber assets of the foundation and any profits arising from these, or any other act in connection with these, shall be exempt from all taxes or charges of any kind, if they relate to the following:

1. Assets located abroad.

2. Any money deposited by either a natural or legal person, whose income does not derive from any Panamanian source or is not taxable in Panama for any reason.

3. Stocks or other securities, which are not issued by any Panamanian corporation or whose income derive from the same, or which are not taxable for any reason, even if these are deposited in the Republic of Panama.

It is important to point out that once the Founder has committed himself to contribute certain assets to the foundation, he is obliged to do so, and the beneficiaries and the foundation will have the right to demand them, even before the courts.

Once the foundation is established, its patrimony can be increased, and this increase does not have to be registered in the Public Registry; therefore, the foundations' real capital will not appear, because after the establishment of the foundation, public knowledge of its patrimony is not required.

BENEFICIARIES

The Beneficiary of the Panamanian Foundation may be a natural person or a corporate body. There may be more than one beneficiary, including the Founder himself/herself. The beneficiary may be determined or generic. In the case of a generic beneficiary, for example, the Founder determines that on a certain date all the associations dealing with cancer research shall benefit from the foundation's assets. Beneficiaries cannot be non-existent and shall be determined in the proper documentation of the Foundation Charter. Beneficiaries of Panamanian Foundations will be selected by a specific method determined in the by-laws. This point is of vital importance to the foundation. It is through this means of designation of the beneficiaries that the existence or the legal grounds of the by-laws are established and this is, in result, the document through which the beneficiaries of the foundation are named. These by-laws are a private document, since it is independent of the Foundation Charter although it is a complementary document. The supervisory body of the Foundation Charter has the power to add or remove beneficiaries of the foundation in accordance to the rules and regulations stipulated in the Foundation Charter and its regulations.

If the beneficiaries are incapacitated in some form or are legally minors, then the legal guardian of these individuals may represent them for the following circumstances:

1. If a judicial proceedings is initiated to remove a member of the Foundation Council because of conflicts of interest with the Founder or beneficiaries of the foundation.

2. If there is any act which has damaged the beneficiaries right of interest to the assets of the foundation and which shall be protested to the supervisory body.

3. If the supervisory body does not exist, the beneficiaries can protest through legal action at the appropriate court in the foundation's domicile.

The heirs of the Founders will have no right after the death of the Founder to annul the foundation or the transfer of assets, even if it has not yet been registered in the Public Registry. The assets may not be subject to any seizures or deemed touchable for any legal reason, except in the case where an injurious action was committed in pursuance of the foundation's goals or of the beneficiaries of the foundation.

Moreover, any "forced heirship" laws in the Founder's domicile shall not affect in any way the validity of the foundation and shall not alter the goals that have been set up in the foundation charter or its regulations.

The Foundation Council shall furnish the beneficiaries and if applicable, to the supervisory entity, all accounts of its administrative work, unless the foundation charter or its regulations state otherwise. If there is no provision regarding the above, then the Foundation Council shall render accounts annually. If the rendered accounts are not objected to by the time specified in the foundation charter or its regulations, the accounts shall be assumed approved by the beneficiaries or supervisory entity. If the foundation charter or its regulations does not specify a time limit for approval, then 90 days from when the accounts were received, shall be the time limit in which the accounts shall be assumed approved by the beneficiaries or supervisory entity

CHARGES, FEES AND TAXES OF THE FOUNDATION

The charge for registering a Panamanian Private Interest Foundation with a capital of B/10,000 is of SIXTY BALBOAS WITH 00/100 (B/60.00) currency of the Republic of Panama.

Panamanian Private Interest Foundations have to pay an annual fee of ONE HUNDRED AND FIFTY BALBOAS WITH 00/100 (B/150) and the charge for delay in the payment will be of THIRTY BALBOAS WITH 00/100 (B/30). This penalty charge will be effective three (3) months after the anniversary of the constitution of the foundation if the fee has not been canceled.

MAIN COMPONENTS OF PANAMANIAN FOUNDATIONS

With exception to the annual fee that every foundation has to pay, the acts of constitution, amendment or liquidation of the foundation, as well as the acts for the transfer, transmission or encumbrance of assets of the foundation and the income from said assets or any other act thereon, will be exempted from all tax, contribution, assessment, encumbrance or payment of any kind or denomination, provided that the assets constitute the following:

1. Assets abroad

2. Money deposited by individuals or legal entities whose income is not Panamanian or not assessable in Panama for any reason

3. Shares or securities of any kind, issued by corporations with non-Panamanian incomes, or when the income is not assessable by any cause, even when said shares or securities have been deposited in the Republic of Panama.

4. Also, transfers of real estate, securities, certificates of deposit, monies or activities pursuant to the purposes of the foundation or by dissolution, in favor of blood relatives of first degree or the spouse of the Founder.

PART IV
GENERAL
DIFFERENCES
BETWEEN
PANAMANIAN AND
LIECHTENSTEIN
FOUNDATIONS

GENERAL DIFFERENCES BETWEEN THE PANAMANIAN FOUNDATION AND LIECHTENSTEIN'S FAMILY FOUNDATION

A quick and descriptive outline of the features or nuances that may exist between the Family Foundation and the Private Interest Foundation are summarized as follows:

First, there is no capital obligation in the Panamanian foundation law. A capital requirement of only USD$10,000 is stipulated while in the Liechtenstein legislation the capital obligation is more stringent with a minimum of 30,000 Swiss Francs required.

Secondly, in the Panamanian Law there is no bookkeeping accountability for holding companies while on the contrary this is an obligation for corporate bodies of any nature in Liechtenstein.

Likewise, the Liechtenstein Foundation has limited liability, which relates to the limit of the capital or of the funds given to the Foundation by the Founder, and bodies are not answerable pursuant to the conception foreseen by the Doctrine and the Law. In comparison the Panamanian Foundation and its bodies have unlimited responsibility pursuant to Panamanian Civil Law.

In the Panamanian Foundation, the heirs cannot attack the assets therein. On the other hand, the Liechtenstein Foundation may be judicially attacked by heirs of the Founder pursuant to Article 560 of the Liechtenstein Act (See Liechtenstein Law, Article 560).

THE PRIVATE INTEREST FOUNDATION OF PANAMA

The Panamanian Foundation does not demand a payment based on capital, and it only requires an annual charge of USD$150. On the contrary, Liechtenstein Foundations imposes a payment of the foundation depending on the capital of the Foundation that depends on the amount to be managed. For example, for more than two million dollars up to ten million dollars it would be _ of one percent and thereafter _ of one percent.

Under Panamanian law there are two ideal types of Foundations: Irrevocable and Revocable Foundations (Article 12), while in the Liechtenstein Family Foundation there are three types of Foundations: Family Foundation, Ecclesiastical Foundation and Mixed Foundation. (Article 553)

In the Panamanian Foundation the parties may establish a supervisory body or committee. In Liechtenstein, the role of the supervisory body is part of the government under Public Law and not in terms of Private Law pursuant to Article 564 of the Liechtenstein Act.

The Panamanian Foundation establishes an international private law section which covers and rules everything pertaining to the change of nationality or new domicile, which in fact is the continuation status, expressed in Articles 28-32. This ensures confidentiality, procedural economy and flexibility in the continuation process. While the Liechtenstein Foundation completely ignores the regulation of law conflicts in its specialized scheme, therefore it would have to resolve these conflicts through Private International Law.

The Liechtenstein Foundation provides the option of transforming a foundation into an Anstalt or Trust Company under the Article 570. Panamanian Law does not have this transformation condition and could prove hazardous in leaving the entity open to controversy involving laws related to trusts.

PART V

LAW 25 OF

JUNE 12, 1995

FOR WHICH REGULATE

THE PRIVATE INTEREST

FOUNDATION

FOR WHICH REGULATE

THE PRIVATE INTEREST FUNDATIONS

ARTICLE 1: One or more natural or juridical persons, acting in their own name or through another, may constitute a private foundation in accordance with the procedures provided in this law. For such purpose, it shall be required the endowment of a patrimony for the purposes expressly provided in the foundation charter. The original endowment may be increased by the creator of the foundation, hereinafter referred to as the Founder, or by any other person.

ARTICLE 2: Private foundations shall be governed by foundation charter, and its regulations, as well as by the provisions of this law and other applicable legal and regulatory provisions. The provisions of Title II of Book I of the Civil Code shall not apply to private foundation.

ARTICLE 3: Private foundations shall not be profit oriented. They may nevertheless engage commercial activities in a non-habitual manner or exercise rights deriving from titles representing the capital of business companies field part of a foundation's assets, provided that economic result or proceeds from such activities are used exclusively towards the foundation's objectives.

THE PRIVATE INTEREST FOUNDATION OF PANAMA

ARTICLE 4: Private foundations may be constituted to become effective at the time of constitution or after the death of their Founder, in either of the following manners:

◆ By private document executed by the Founder whose signature shall be authenticated by a notary public at the place of constitution.

◆ Directly before a notary public at the place of constitution.

In either case, the constitution of the foundation shall comply with the formalities established in the present law for the creation of foundations.

In the case of a foundation being created to become effective after the death of the Founder, whether by public or private document, the formalities required for the execution of wills shall not apply.

ARTICLE 5: The foundation charter shall contain:

1) The name of the foundation in any language with characters of the Latin alphabet, and which shall not be identical or similar to that of any other foundation previously existing in the Republic of Panama, to avoid confusion. The name shall include the word foundation to distinguish it from a natural person or from a different kind of juridical person.

2) The initial capital of the foundation, expressed in any currency of legal tender, and which shall in no case be less than an amount equivalent to ten thousand Balboas (B/. 10,000.00).

3) A complete and clear designation of the member or members of the Foundation Council, to which the Founder may belong, including their addresses.

4) The domicile of the foundation.

5) The name and domicile of the resident agent of the foundation in the Republic of Panama, who must be an attorney or law firm. The resident agent must countersign the foundation charter prior to its registration at the Public Registry.

6) The purposes or objects of the foundation.

7) The manner of appointing the beneficiaries of the foundation, which may include the Founder.

8) The reservation of the right to modify the foundation charter when deemed convenient.

9) The duration of the foundation.

10) The destination to be given to the estate of the foundation and the manner of liquidating such estate in the event of dissolution.

11) Any other Lawful clauses which, the Founder may consider convenient.

ARTICLE 6: The foundation charter, as well as any amendment thereto, may be drafted in any language with charm of the Latin alphabet, and must comply with regulations regarding registration of acts and at the Public Registry, for which purpose it first be protocolized by a notary public of the Republic of Panama. If the foundation charter or amendments are not written in Spanish, they shall be protocolized together with its Spanish translation made by a certified public translator of the Republic of Panama.

ARTICLE 7: Any amendments, to the foundation charter, when permitted, shall be executed and signed in accordance to the provisions of the foundation charter itself. The relevant agreement, resolution or act of amendment shall contain the date in which it was carried out, and a clear indication of the name of the person or persons executing such amendments, whose signatures shall likewise be authenticated by a notary public at the place of execution of the document.

ARTICLE 8: Every private foundation shall pay registration fees and annual taxes equivalent to those established for corporations in the Articles 318 and 318A of the Fiscal Code.

The procedure and form of payment, the surcharge for late payment, the consequences of non-payment, as well as all the complementary dispositions of the legal precepts previously cited will also be applicable to private foundations.

ARTICLE 9: The registration of the foundation charter of private foundation at the Public Registry shall confer upon it juridical personality without the need for any other legal or administrative authorization. Registration at the Public Registry shall in addition constitute a mean of publicity with regard to third parties. Consequently, a foundation may acquire and own assets of all kinds, incur obligations and be a party to administrative and judicial proceedings of any order, in accordance with any applicable legal provisions.

ARTICLE 10: Once a Foundation has acquired juridical personality, the Founder or any third party who has acquired an obligation to contribute assets to the foundation, either by himself/herself or at the request of another person with interest in the foundation, shall formalize the transfer to the foundation of the assets which they agreed to transfer. When the foundation is constituted to be effective at the time of death of its Founder, it shall be deemed to have existed prior to the death of the Founder with respect to the donations, which he/she may have made to the foundation.

ARTICLE 11: The assets of the Foundation shall constitute an estate separate from the Founder's personal assets for all legal purposes, and may not be seized or attached or be subject to any precautionary action or measure, except in the case of obligations incurred, or damages caused by virtue of actions taken fulfilling the purposes or objectives of the foundation, or of legitimate rights of the beneficiaries of the foundation. In no case shall such assets be affected or used to respond for the personal obligations of the Founder or of the beneficiaries.

ARTICLE 12: Foundations shall be irrevocable except in the following cases:

1) If the foundation charter has not been registered at the Public Registry.

2) When the foundation charter provides otherwise.

3) For any of the causes of revocation applicable to donations.

The transfers of assets made to foundations shall be irrevocable by the person who made the transfer, unless it is expressly stated otherwise in the act of transference of such assets.

ARTICLE 13: In addition to the foregoing provisions, when a foundation has been created to be effective the time of death of its Founder, he/she shall have the exclusive and unlimited right to revoke.

The heirs of the Founder, after his/her death, shall have no right to revoke the creation or transfer of assets to the foundation, even when it has been registered at the Public Registry before death of the Founder.

ARTICLE 14: The existence of legal provisions regarding inheritance at the place of domicile of the Founder or of the beneficiaries shall not affect the foundation or its validity, and shall not prevent the attainment of its purposes in the manner provided in the foundation charter or its regulations.

ARTICLE 15: The creditors of the Founder or of a third party shall have the right to contest the contribution or transfer of assets to a foundation when such transfer constitutes an act in fraud of the creditors. The rights and actions of such creditors shall lapse at the expiration of three (3) years, counted from the date of the contribution or transfer of the assets to the foundation.

ARTICLE 16: The patrimony of the foundation may originate from any lawful business and may consist of assets of any kind, present or future. The Founder or third parties may periodically incorporate other sums of money or assets to the estate. The transfer of assets to the estate of the foundation may be effected by public or private document, provided however that, in the case of immovable property, the transfer shall comply with the rules for the transfer of such property.

ARTICLE 17: The foundation shall have a Foundation Council whose powers or responsibilities shall be established in the foundation charter in its regulations. Unless the Council is a juridical person, the number of members of the Foundation Council shall be no less than three (3).

ARTICLE 18: The Foundation Council shall be responsible for carrying out the purposes or objectives of the foundation. Unless the foundation charter or its regulations provide otherwise, the Foundation Council shall have the following general obligations and duties:

1) To administer the assets of the foundation in accordance with the foundation charter or its regulations.

2) To carry out acts, contracts or lawful businesses which are convenient or necessary to advance the purposes of the foundation, and

to include in such contracts, agreements and other instruments or obligations such clauses and conditions as are necessary or convenient and not contrary to the law, to bonos mores, or to public order and which are in accordance with the purposes of the foundation.

3) To inform the beneficiaries of the foundation of the economic situation of the same as provided by the foundation charter or its regulations.

4) To deliver to the beneficiaries of the foundation the assets, properties or resources designated for them by the foundation charter or its regulations.

5) To carry out all such acts or contracts which are permitted to the foundation by the present law and by other applicable or regulatory provisions.

ARTICLE 19: The foundation charter or its regulations may provide that, in order to exercise their powers, the members of the Foundation Council must obtain the previous authorization of a protector, committee or other supervisory entity appointed by the Founder or the majority of the Founders. The members of the Foundation Council shall not be held liable for the loss or deterioration of the assets of the foundation or for the damages caused by their decisions, provided that the above mentioned authorization has been duly obtained.

ARTICLE 20: Unless the foundation charter or its regulations provide otherwise, the Foundation Council must render accounts of its administration to the beneficiaries and, where applicable, to the supervisory entity. If the foundation charter or its regulations contain no provision in this regard, the rendering of accounts must be done annually. If the accounts so rendered not objected with in the time specified in the foundation charter or its regulations, or, if the charter does not regulate the matter, within ninety (90) days from the date the accounts were received, they shall be deemed to have been approved, for which purpose the above mentioned period of ninety (90) days must be indicated in the report rendering the accounts. On the lapse of such period or upon the approval of the accounts, the members of the Foundation Council shall be free of liability for their administration, unless they bad failed to act with the diligence of a bonus paterfamilias. The above mentioned approval does not exonerate the members of the Foundation Council vis-a-vis the beneficiaries or third parties having an interest in the foundation with respect to damages caused by gross negligence or fraud in the administration of the foundation.

ARTICLE 21: The Founder may reserve for himself/herself or for other persons, in the foundation charter, the right to remove the members of the Foundation Council as well as the right to designate or add new members.

ARTICLE 22: If the foundation charter or its regulations contain no provision regarding the right and causes for removal of the members of the Foundation Council, said members may be removed by means of summary juridical proceedings for the following causes:

1) When the interests are in compatible with the interests of the beneficiaries of the Founder.

2) If they do not administer the assets of the foundation with the diligence of a bonus paterfamilias.

3) If they are convicted of crane against private property or public faith. In such case, while the criminal proceedings are taking place, the temporary suspension of the member on trial may be decreed.

4) For incapacity or impossibility to carry out the objectives of the foundation from the time such causes arise.

5) For insolvency or bankruptcy proceedings.

ARTICLE 23: The judicial removal of the members of Foundation Council may be requested by the Founder and the beneficiary or beneficiaries. If beneficiaries were disabled or minors, they may be represented by whoever exercise patriae potestas or legal guardianship over them, as the case may be.

The judgment of the court decreasing the removal shall also appoint new members to replace the form who must be persons with sufficient capacity, qualifications and recognized moral standing administer the assets of the foundation, in accordance with the purposes established by the Founder.

ARTICLE 24: The foundation charter or its regulations may provide for the constitution of supervisory bodies which may be composed of natural or juridical persons, such as auditing companies, protector of foundation, or other similar entities.

The powers of the supervisory entities shall be established in the foundation charter or its regulations, and may include, among others the following:

1) To ensure the fulfillment of the foundation's purposes by the Foundation Council and protect the rights and interests of the beneficiaries.

2) To require the Foundation Charter to render accounts.

3) To modify the objects and purposes of the foundation when their fulfillment becomes impossible or too burdensome.

4) To appoint new members of the Foundation Council by reason of temporary or permanent absence, or for the expiration of the period which they were appointed.

5) To appoint new member of the Foundation Council in replacement of existing members in the event of temporary or accidental absence of any of them.

6) To increase or reduce the number of members of the Foundation Council.

7) To approve the acts done by the Foundation Council pursuant to the foundation charter or its regulations.

8) To act as custodians of the assets of the foundation and to oversee the application thereof to the objects or purposes contained in the foundation charter.

To remove beneficiaries of the foundation and to add new beneficiaries, in accordance with the provisions of the foundation charter or its regulations.

ARTICLE 25: The foundation shall be dissolved:

1) On the date in which the foundation must come to an end in accordance with the foundation charter.

2) On the accomplishment of the ends or purposes for which it was created or if their fulfillment becomes impossible.

3) If it becomes insolvent, incapable of making payments or it has been Judicially declared to be subject to bankruptcy proceedings.

4) On the loss or total extinction of the assets of the foundation.

5) On its revocation.

For any other reason established in foundation charter or in the present law.

ARTICLE 26: Any beneficiary of the foundation may object acts of the foundation which damage his or her right or interests by denouncing such circumstance to the protector or other supervisory body; if any, or if there are none, by directly instituting corresponding judicial action before the appropriate court of the domicile of the foundation.

ARTICLE 27: The acts of constitution, amendment or extinction of the foundation, as well as the acts of transfer, transmittal or encumbrance of assets of the Foundation and the income arising therefrom or any other act in connection therewith, shall be exempt from all taxes, contributions, duties, liens, or assessments of any kind, provided they relate to:

1) Assets located abroad.

2) Money deposited by natural or juridical persons whose incomes do not derive from Panamanian source or is not taxable in Panama for any reason.

3) Shares or securities of any kind issued by corporations in which income is not derived from a Panamanian source, or which are not taxable for any reason, even when such shares or securities are deposited in the Republic of Panama.

The transfer of immovable property, titles, certificates of deposit, assets, funds, securities or shares carried out by reason of the fulfillment of the objectives of the foundation or the termination of the same, in favor of relatives within the first degree of consanguinity or the spouse of the Founder shall also be exempted from all taxes.

ARTICLE 28: Foundations organized in accordance with a foreign law may become subject to the provisions of this law.

ARTICLE 29: Foundations referred to in the preceding article that elect to become subject to the provisions of this law shall present a certificate of continuation, issued by the corresponding body or organ of the foundation which according to its own internal organization shall issue the same, and which shall contain:

1) The name of the foundation and the date of its constitution.

2) Data about the registration or deposit of the instrument at the registry of the country of origin.

3) An express declaration of its desire to continue its legal existence as a Panamanian foundation.

4) The requirements of article 5 of this law for the constitution of Panamanian private foundations.

ARTICLE 30: The certificate of continuation and the other requirements mentioned in the preceding article should have the following documents attached to them:

1) Copy of the original act of constitution of the foundation that desires to continue as a Panamanian foundation, together with any subsequent amendment.

2) Power of attorney extended to a Panamanian lawyer to carry out the necessary procedures to effect the continuation of the foundation in Panama.

ARTICLE 31: In the cases provided for in article 28, the responsibilities, duties and rights acquired prior to the change of jurisdiction of the foundation, as well as proceedings brought against it or those brought by the foundation, shall continue in effect, and such rights and obligations shall not be affected by the change of jurisdiction authorized by the aforementioned legal provisions.

ARTICLE 32: Foundations constituted in accordance with this law, as well as the assets which constitute their patrimony, may transfer or become subject to the laws and jurisdiction of another country, as may be provided by their foundation charter or their regulations.

ARTICLE 33: Registrations concerning private foundations shall be made at the Public Registry in a special section to be known as "Sections of Private Foundations". The Executive Branch of Government, acting through the Ministry of Government and Justice, shall issue the regulations applicable to such section.

ARTICLE 34: To avoid the undue use of private foundations all the provisions in Executive Decree No. 468 of 1994 and any other legal disposition in force aimed at combating money laundering arising from drug trafficking shall be applied to their operations.

ARTICLE 35: All members of the Foundation Council and of the supervisory bodies, if any, as well as public or private employees, who have any knowledge of the activities, transactions or operations of the foundations, must at all times bold the same in secret and confidentiality. Breaches of this duty shall be sanctioned with imprisonment of six months and a fine of fifty thousand Balboas (B/. 50,000.00), without prejudice to the corresponding civil liability.

The provisions of this article are applicable without prejudice to the information that must be disclosed to official authorities and the inspections the latter must carry out in the manner established by the law.

ARTICLE 36: Any controversy for which no special procedure is specified in the present law shall be resolved by summary proceedings.

The foundation charter or its regulations may establish that an arbitrator or arbitrators, as well as the procedure to be followed thereby shall resolve any controversy arising in connection with the foundation. In the event no such procedure has been established, the statutes ruling such matters as contained in the Judicial Code shall apply.

ARTICLE 37: This law shall enter into force after its promulgation.

Note: this law has been translated into English from the Spanish version of the foundation law.

PART VI
LIECHTENSTEIN
COMPANY LAW
THE ESTABLISHMENT
AND FOUNDATIONS

FIFTH TITLE

THE ESTABLISHMENT AND FOUNDATIONS

FIRST SECTION

THE ESTABLISHMENTS

Art. 534

An establishment within the intendment of this title and pursuant to the following regulations is a legally autonomous, organized, permanent undertaking dedicated to economic or other objects and entered on the Public Register as the Establishment Register, which has holdings of material and possibly personal resources. It does not have the character of an institution under public law and has no other form of legal entity.

Establishments under public law which serve a defined permanent object and are in the hands of the public administration are subject to public law, insofar as exceptions do not exist and, where they are independent, to the following regulations supplementally.

Ecclesiastical establishments are subject to public law and, supplementally, cannon law.

Establishments without legal personality (non-independent establishments) and other non-independently donated assets for a specific object are not subject to the following regulations, but to the regulations concerning the implied trust. Foundations are reserved.

Art. 535

An establishment may be formed and operated by an individual person, or firm, a community or by an association of communes or a legal entity not otherwise entered in the Public Register.

Communes and associations of communes require Government assent to the formation.

More than one Founder is not required.

Art. 536

Written articles are necessary for the formation, signed by one or several Founders.

Moreover, the articles of an establishment must contain provisions concerning the following:

1. The name and/ or the name of the firm, the domicile and the designation as "Establishment",

2. The objects of the establishment,

3. The estimated value of the establishment capital in the event that it is not in cash and the manner of procurement and composition,

4. The powers of the supreme body,

5. The bodies for the administration and if necessary for the auditing and the manner in which representation is implemented,

6. The principles relating to the drawing up of the balance sheet and the appropriation of the surplus,

7. The form in which the establishment's notices ensue.

With the exception of Nos. 6 and 7 these provisions shall be deemed to be essential pursuant to the regulations concerning voidablility.

Where the establishment capital exists in a form other than cash, the endowed assets may, instead of in the articles, be entered in detail in a special register, which must be deposited with the Register Office for safe keeping.

Like a company limited by shares, an Establishment may also be formed with a variable capital. This circumstance must be entered in the Public Register.

Art. 537

If the law does not provide otherwise, all establishments are required to be entered in the Public Register.

A certified copy of the articles and documented proof of donation of capital must be enclosed with the application to register, which must contain:

1. The formation deed (the resolution and/or declaration of formation) in the event that it is not already included in the articles,

2. The declaration that at least half the establishment capital has been paid in or covered by payment in kind and stating how the remainder is to be raised and/or secured,

3. A list of the members of the board of directors stating the names of the members, their place of residence and/or the name of the firm and domicile.

Art. 538

The following shall be entered in the Public Register and published as an extract:

1. The formation deed, if this is not included in the articles,

2. The date of the articles,

3. The name and/or the name of the firm and the domicile of the establishment,

4. The objects of the undertaking and, if applicable, the duration of the establishment,

5. The amount of capital endowed to the establishment as well as the sum paid in or the other assets contributed, with their estimated value,

6. If applicable, the participation rights of third parties in particular, in addition to the entitled beneficiaries,

7. The name, first name and place of residence and/or the name of the firm and domicile of the members of the boards of directors, the form in which the board of directors gives notice of its expressions of intent and the manner of representation.

8. The form in which the establishment's announcements shall ensue. The establishment comes into existence and acquires legal personality upon entry in the Public Register. Should action be taken on behalf of the establishment before the said establishment has acquired or without it having legal personality, the parties acting on behalf of the establishment, in particular Founders or persons al-

ready appointed as governing bodies shall be liable pursuant to the general regulations concerning legal entities.

Art. 539

The establishment capital (endowment fund) may be endowed either completely or up to a partial amount to be determined in the articles in funds contributed by the Founders who, however, shall have no claim interest at a determined level.

The fund contributions must be paid in or contributed within the period of time determined in the articles.

Where the Founders bring items of property into the establishment which are to be credited to the fund contributions, the articles or the register shall establish individually, in detail, accurately and completely the object contributed, its expert valuation and any beneficial interests which may be tied thereto.

Should the establishment capital be paid in full or covered by means of assets at a later date when the establishment is in operation, this fact shall be registered in the Public Register.

Art. 540

Establishment shares of the establishment assets for the Founders or third parties shall only exist pursuant to the regulation of the articles, even though fund contributions have been effected and entitled beneficiaries have been designated to draw profit from the establishment.

Shares and share certificates of an establishment shall also be null and void as long as the admissibility of shares or share certificates is not provided for in the articles and the issuer and third party participants shall be liable pursuant to the provisions drawn up under the general regulations.

In case of doubt, the shares provided for the Founders in the articles shall be in proportion to the amount of their possible fund contributions and if funds have not been contributed the Founders shall receive equal shares.

Establishment shares shall be treated as securities only when the articles make express provision for such treatment.

Establishment certificates as securities shall be subject to the regulations concerning registered shares unless more restrictive regulations concerning their transferability are drawn up in the articles.

The board of directors shall keep a register of the establishment shares with appropriate application of the regulations concerning the share register in the case of a limited liability company.

Art. 541

The Founder's rights to which one or several persons are entitled may be relinquished or otherwise transferred or inherited but may not be pledged or otherwise charged.

Art. 542

The contestation of an establishment by the heirs or the creditors of a Founder shall ensue, if it was formed in favor of third party beneficiaries without valuable consideration, as in the case of a gift.

Art. 543

The bearer(s) of Founder's rights form(s) the establishment's supreme body. The articles may also confer the powers of the supreme body upon the board of directors.

Where the law or the articles do not determine to the contrary, the supreme body shall be entitled to those powers which are provided by the general provisions for the supreme body.

Where several persons have Founder's rights, resolutions shall require the assent of all bearers of Founder's rights in order to be valid if the articles do not determine otherwise.

A bearer of Founder's rights shall be at liberty to represent personally the Founder's rights to which he is entitled or to instruct a third party, who is not required to be a bearer of Founder's rights, by means of a written power of attorney to represent the said Founder's rights.

Art. 544

The members of the board of directors are not required to entitled beneficiaries.

If the law or the articles do not determine otherwise, the judge may, upon application of the participants, in extra judicial proceedings, appoint the members of the board of directors in case of doubt for a period of three years and remove them or individual members at any time, without prejudice to claims for compensation.

In the absence of a deviating provision, the board of directors shall be under obligation to the establishment also to observe all those restrictions which, upon application of the participants, are determined by the judge in extra judicial proceedings, relating to the scope of their authority, the conduct of establishment business and the representation of the establishment. However, a restriction on representation towards bone fide third parties shall have legal effect only insofar as the law permits this.

Where an audit authority board is prescribed pursuant to the general regulations or the articles make provision for this, the judge may, in extra judicial proceedings, in the absence of another provision in the law or the articles, appoint or remove the audit authority, in the same way as the members of the board of directors are appointed or removed.

Art. 545

The articles shall determine in detail:

◆ Who shall benefit from the establishment and its possible net profit (beneficiaries),

◆ The manner in which these shall be determined specifically,

◆ Whether and in what way the beneficiaries shall be entitled to participate in the organization (supreme body, board of directors, supervision).

As long as no third parties have been appointed as beneficiaries (entitled beneficiaries), it shall be assumed that the bearer of the Founder's rights is the beneficiary.

Only an amount corresponding to the surplus of net assets in excess of the establishment capital paid-in pursuant to the articles or otherwise covered may be withdrawn from the establishment assets as available net profit, after allowance has been made for possible reserves to be paid into the reserve fund provided for in the articles.

Upon the demand of the board of directors, unknown beneficiaries may be called in public citation proceedings on condition that individual performances which have not been withdrawn shall become forfeited in favor of the regional public assistance fund three years after the call, unless the articles determine otherwise.

Art. 546

In the case of family establishments, the Founder may determine in the articles that the establishment beneficial interest \of the specifically designated third parties, acquired without valuable consideration, may not be withdrawn from them by their creditors by way of levy of execution and writ or by bankruptcy proceedings initiated against them. This circumstance shall be annotated in the Public Register at the time of registration.

Apart from the previously mentioned provision in the articles, the income received without valuable consideration by a third party beneficiary from an establishment formed by another may be withdrawn from the said third party by creditors by way of levy of execution and writ or bankruptcy proceedings, only if the said income is not required for the defrayal of the essential maintenance of the beneficiary, the beneficiary's spouse and children not provided for.

Art. 547

Where the articles do not determine to the contrary, the book value of the establishment assets shall be determined from the difference between the valuation of the assets, undertaken annually, and the debts owed to third parties.

Under these circumstances, the annual balance sheet shall show the amount by which the establishment assets have increased or diminished by comparison with the previous business year.

In this case, only the amount yielded during the course of the year may be distributed as profit after the deduction of any reserves that may have to be formed.

Art. 548

In all cases, only the establishment's assets shall be liable for the establishment's debts.

Each Founder shall only be required to meet the obligation to transfer as specified the endowed assets including a limited liability or liability to make further contributions as in the case of registered cooperative societies. The Founder shall not be released from these performances nor may respite be granted and this shall apply in the event of the bankruptcy of the establishment.

Instead of or in absence of members, third parties may also assume the limited liability for the establishment's obligations or a limited liability to make further contributions.

Art. 549

The Founder may at any time amend the articles and, in particular, the objects, with reservation of the creditors' rights, e.g., by increasing or reducing the establishment of capital, changing the governing bodies and by making other similar amendments.

Instead of or in addition to the Founder, the articles may empower other persons, legal entities, firms or authorities to amend the articles and include detailed regulations concerning this.

Where the Founder's rights cannot exercised and the articles do not determine otherwise, they may be amended by the judge in extra judicial proceedings upon application by the board of directors or one of the beneficiaries, taking into consideration the objects of the establishment.

Art. 550

To what extent the dissolution of a legal entity, a company or a firm which is the Founder or possessor of an establishment results I the dissolution of the said establishment shall be pronounced by the judge in the individual case, after considering all the circumstances.

Insofar as the law concerning establishments or the articles do not indicate a deviation, the relevant regulations concerning registered cooperative societies shall be applied accordingly to the take-over of one establishment by another and the association of several establishments.

The regulations concerning the conversion of a company limited by shares in the case of limited liability companies shall be applied accordingly to the conversion to an establishment of a company limited by shares or a company with limited liability.

Art. 551

If no mandatory regulations are drawn up in this section and no or no satisfactory rule is contained herein, the regulations concerning trust enterprises with legal personality shall be applied, in addition to the general regulations concerning legal entities.

For establishments without members which serve exclusively non-profit making purposes, the supplementary regulations concerning the supervision, conversion and cancellation of a foundation shall apply, and for family establishments without members the regulations for family foundations, provided that a deviation is not foreseen in this section or in the articles.

SECOND SECTION

THE FOUNDATIONS

Art. 552

For a foundation to be formed by natural persons or legal entities or firms, it is necessary for assets to be endowed (foundation property) for a certain specific purpose. Ecclesiastical, family and no-profit making purposes may be given particular consideration. Commercial activities may by undertaken by a foundation only provided such activity serves its noncommercial purpose or the type and scope of the participation's held require the facilities of a commercial business.

Asset donations without legal personality (dependent foundations) or donations tied to the condition of a special administration under a special name and of application for a special purpose and similar conditions to already existing legal entities or natural persons or companies are subject to special regulations such as those applying to gifts or concerning the law of succession and, supplementary, to the regulations concerning the implied trust relationship.

The judge shall decide in the individual case the extent to which separately administered assets (fund) shall be entitled to independence according to private law or to the character of trust property.

The regulations concerning the enterprise with legal personality shall be applied to foundations accordingly, particularly with regard to foundation participants (Founder, foundation council, beneficiaries), where and insofar as the following provisions or the foundation articles or the regulations concerning the obligation of trust enterprises to register do not determine to the contrary.

Art. 553

Ecclesiastical foundations within the intendment of this section are foundations formed for ecclesiastical purposes.

A family foundation is a pure family foundation where the foundation assets are continuously connected with the purpose of defraying the expenses for the upbringing and education, outfitting or support of the relatives of one or several designated families, or with similar purposes.

It is a mixed foundation where assets so donated serve ecclesiastical or other purposes outside the family in addition or supplementally.

Art. 554

To ensure observance of the obligation to register, to prevent foundations with unlawful or immoral purposes and to avoid circumvention of
possible supervision, the foundation deed and/or a certified copy of
the testamentary disposition or the deed of inheritance must be deposited by the foundation council or the legal representative and/or the
probate court with the Register Office at the time a foundation is formed,
insofar as an application for entry does not ensue otherwise. Amendments of the articles must also be deposited with the Register Office.

Art. 555

The formation of a foundation ensues in the form of a deed on which
the signatures of the Founders are certified, by testamentary disposition
or by deed of inheritance.

The foundation deed or the articles must contain the name and domicile of the foundation, its purpose or object, the designation of the
foundation council members and the method for appointing another
foundation council as well as a provision concerning the application of
the assets in the event of the dissolution of the foundation.

Art. 556

The foundation's application to register in the foundation Register must
be recorded by all the members of the foundation council personally or
submitted in writing in certified form. A certified copy of the foundation deed must accompany the application.

The entry and publication, which may ensue by announcement on the
court notice board, must contain: the name, (name of the firm), address
and purpose of the foundation, the date of the formation deed, the

names and addresses and/or the name and domicile of the firm of the foundation council members and/or of other representatives.

If necessary, entry and publication may also be undertaken by order of the Government s supervising authority by virtue of the foundation deed, possibly by the Register Authority ex officio upon notification by the Probate Authority or upon petition of the beneficiaries.

Art. 557

The foundation only comes into existence when entered in the Public Register as foundation Register.

Ecclesiastical foundations, pure and mixed family foundations and foundations whose entitled beneficiaries are specifically designated or definable acquire legal personality without being entered in the Public Register.

Foundations that engage in commercial activities are under the obligation to register and acquire legal personality only when entered in the Public Register.

The registration of a foundation formed by testamentary disposition shall ensue only after the death of the Founder and, in the case of a deed on inheritance, provided hat this does not determine otherwise, only after the death of one of the Founders.

Art. 558

When the foundation has come into existence, the Founder or the third party, upon demand of the Supervising Authority, the representative of public law or of interested parties, is required to transfer to the foundation the assets mentioned in the deed of the foundation.

Rights, for whose transfer a declaration of assignment is sufficient, devolve by operation of the law upon the foundation on coming into existence.

Where the foundation only becomes effective on the death of the Founder or after the termination of a firm or legal entity, the said foundation shall be deemed to have been in existence already before the death or termination of the Founder for the donations of the Founder or third party.

The donation of assets may also be effected, in particular, by the establishment of a contractual relationship to the Founder or third party according to which the Founder or third party undertakes to donate annually or at certain intervals a fixed or variable sum or other assets (donation of periodical payments).

In case of doubt, the investment of assets shall ensue pursuant to the regulations concerning trust investments.

Art. 559

Revocation of the foundation is admissible only:

1. If a foundation has not yet been entered in the Public Register, inasmuch as existence ensues only in the event of such entry,

2. In the event that registration of the foundation is not necessary and the foundation should become effective in law during the Founder's lifetime, up to the time of conclusion of registration,

3. In the case of foundations formed by testamentary disposition or deed of inheritance, pursuant to the regulations of the laws of succession applicable to these circumstances.

4. In the case of testamentary dispositions, the Founder personally has an unrestricted right of revocation but not, on the other hand, the heirs after the Founder's death, not even if the foundation is not yet entered in the Public Register.

Likewise, the heirs do not have a right of revocation where in the case of the foundation inter vivos the Founder certainly drew up the deed but died before the foundation was entered in the Public Register.

Revocation expressly reserved in the foundation deed or the reserved amendment of the deed or of the articles is admissible at any time.

Art. 560

The heirs or the creditors may dispute the validity of a foundation in the same way as a gift.

Also after it has been registered, the Founder and his heirs may dispute the validity of the foundation on grounds of deficiency of intention in the manner admissible pursuant to the provisions of contract law.

Art. 561

The foundation's governing bodies, such as the foundation council, the audit authority and similar bodies, s well as the type of administration and representation, etc., are determined in the deed of foundation or in the foundation articles drawn up by the Founder in a document, a will or a deed of inheritance.

The conferment of beneficial interest in the foundation may be entrusted to a special body (collators), independently of the foundation council.

The regulations concerning the governing bodies in question in the case of establishments shall be applied accordingly to the powers and duties of the bodies appointed I this manner, with reservation of the following provisions.

Art. 562

Where no governing bodies have been provided for or where those provided are inadequate, the Supervising Authority shall take the necessary steps with appropriate observance of the regulations concerning the establishments governing bodies. If required, the Supervising Authority shall arrange for entry in the Public Register.

In the event that such steps cannot be taken expeditiously if, for instance, there are inadequate assets, the Supervising Authority, provided the founder does not object or a provision of the foundation deed or the foundation articles is not expressly opposed to this, shall donate the assets on trust to another foundation having as far as possible the same kind of purpose.

Art. 563

Only the foundation's assets shall be liable for the foundation's debts to the creditors.

Except for the extensive provisions in the case of family foundations, income which a person receives from a foundation without valuable consideration may be withdrawn by injunction, levy of execution and writ or bankruptcy proceedings only when the said income is not required for the defrayal of the essential living expenses of the beneficiary, his spouse and his children without means.

In the case of foundations subject to supervision, unknown beneficiaries of the foundation may be traced by the Government or, otherwise, upon application by the judge in public citation proceedings.

Art. 564

With the exception of ecclesiastical foundations, pure and mixed family foundations or such foundations as those whose entitled beneficiaries are specifically designated or definable natural or juridical persons, firms or their successors in title or those foundations whose purpose is solely to administer the assets and distribute the income, participation or similar, the foundations are subject to supervision by the Government, which shall be notified by the Public Register Authority of every foundation under obligation to register.

The foundation deed may also subject other foundations to Government supervision.

It shall be incumbent upon the Supervising Authority to ensure that the foundation assets are administered and applied pursuant to their purposes. This Supervising Authority may give the necessary orders concerning, for example, auditing and the dismissal of the foundations' governing bodies.

Any person who has an interest I the administration and application of the assets, their yield or use and the representative of public law may lodge a complaint with the Supervisory Authority concerning an administration and application of the assets by the foundation" bodies which is, in conflict with the purpose of the foundation.

The participants shall be heard before a decision is pronounced by the Supervising Authority or the Administrative Court of Justice.

Art. 565

After hearing the foundation's supreme authority and those persons whose rights are affected, the Government, upon application of one of the participants or ex officio, may change the foundation's organization by administrative action if this is required urgently in order to preserve the assets or safeguard the foundation's purpose and insofar as the foundation deed or the articles has (have) not entrusted another body or a third party with the changing of the organization.

The Supervising Authority may designate the Landensbank in particular as a foundation governing body.

In opposition to such amendment orders, the participants may lodge an appeal with the Administrative court.

Art. 566

After hearing the foundation's supreme authority and those persons whose rights are affected, the Government, upon application by participants or ex officio, may amend the foundation deed by administrative action if its original purpose has acquired a completely different meaning or effect and as a result of this the foundation is obviously estranged from the intentions of the Founder.

The foundation deed or the articles may also provide for a foundation governing body or a third party to be empowered to effect amendment of the purpose if its is incapable of achievement, inadmissible or unreasonable.

Charges and conditions that impair the foundation's purpose may be cancelled or amended under the same preconditions.

The last paragraph of the preceding article shall be applied accordingly.

Art. 567

Permanent or temporary judicial supervision with respect to the regulation of the governing bodies and the purpose of foundations not subject to supervision, insofar as ecclesiastical foundations are not concerned, and their conversion may, upon application of participants, be pronounced by the judge in extrajudicial proceedings and, if adequate reasons exist, be cancelled again. In this case, the judge, like the Government as Supervising Authority, may give the necessary instructions.

If provision has not been made for the absolute discretion of the foundation's governing bodies, the judge shall in all cases decide in contentious proceedings concerning other difficulties of a private law nature such as, for example, the question of beneficial interest (entitlements or privilege), its scope, and so forth.

In the case of family foundations, the Founder may determine at the same time that the creditors of the specifically designated third party beneficiaries shall not withdraw from these their beneficial interest acquired without valuable consideration by way of injunction, levy of execution and writ or bankruptcy proceedings.

Trust certificates may also be issued to the entitled beneficiaries.

Art. 568

The cancellation of a foundation ensues by operation of the law as soon as the purpose cannot be achieved, particularly when the foundation purpose can no longer be realized when, owing to lack of adequate assets, the duties of the foundation can no longer be fulfilled or the duration specified in the foundation deed has expired.

Art. 569

The Supervising Authority, the representative of public law and any interested party is entitled to take action.

The cancellation shall be reported to the Registrar ex officio in order that deregistration may ensue.

The action may be annotated in the Public Register before or during the proceedings, up to the time of final decision, upon application or ex officio. The governing bodies of the foundation and other participants shall be heard before the decision is made.

Art. 570

Where conversion is expressly provided for and also the necessary prerequisites, such as articles or governing bodies are provided, the foundation, without being wound up, may be converted by the foundation council or a third party empowered by the foundation council into an establishment or a trust enterprise by means of a document which must be correct with respect to form.

PART VII
THE HARRIS
ORGANISATION

THE HARRIS ORGANISATION

Today, the Harris Organisation™[1] is the largest independent pro
vider of quality international financial services in Latin America
and the Caribbean, with more than 150 employees and a holding company with paid up capital in excess of US $10 million. Our firm
offers clients offshore investment opportunities and asset protection,
with an emphasis on tax and estate planning. Clients of The Firm of
Marc M. Harris include banks, brokerage houses, large accounting firms
and government institutions. Still, the most valued customers are individuals.

During our survey in The Americas, it became apparent that one of
the biggest items individuals wanted was the ability to create corporations, foundations and trusts within a matter of hours. Our Firm offers
specialized services that delivers timely solutions for any individual's
asset protection needs.

The basic structure that we construct for individuals consists of a
foundation, trust and corporation. The Panamanian Family Foundations is our response to recent legislation activated in the Republic of
Panama. A Panamanian Corporation, owned by the Foundation, is the
vehicle through which the client's investments are made.

---

1 The Harris Organisation is a fully owned trademark of Marc M. Harris et Cie., 1 BVI Holding Company.

The structure functions by removing the majority of assets from the client's estate through transfers to foundations. Without assets, clients may favorably alter their tax liabilities.

In addition to offering asset protection, the Firm also specializes in mutual fund administration. At present, we manage over 80 in-house mutual funds as well as a score of outside funds. The Harris Group of Funds invests in a wide variety of industries and markets, specializing in the natural resource sector.

As a full service provider of international financial planning, we offer individuals the following range of services:

◆ Creation of International Fiduciary Structures, including detailed tax, estate, financial and business planning;

◆ Analysis of commercial operations to maximize wealth;

◆ Total administration of all entities and fulfillment of legal requirements;

◆ Preparation of all domestic and foreign documents, and income tax returns;

◆ Nominee services;

◆ Complete international investment services;

◆ True international investment products made available only to offshore investors, through our own full-service discount brokerage department and our association with the largest international banks in the world; and

◆ Access to investment in stocks, bonds, mutual funds, precious metals, oil and gas.

OUR MANIFESTO

The most rapidly growing offshore service providers of tomorrow are all man-made financial industries that can be physically located anywhere on the face of the earth. Where they will be located depends on who organizes the brainpower to capture them. The Harris Organisation is well placed to be the headquarters and advisor for those who hope to be on the forefront of this international globalization of financial services

Modern transportation costs have created a world where both physical and human resources can be cheaply moved to wherever they are needed. Market availability has also fallen out of the competitive equation. With the development of a world capital market, everyone essentially invests in New York, London, or Tokyo.

Today, an investor in Peru can invest in hundreds of global mutual funds via Panama's financial center as any other market player in the United States, Germany, or Japan despite his living in a country with a per capita income that is a fraction of the Big 3 economic powers. In short, there will be no advantage of investing from a capital-rich or capital-poor country.

Panama's financial center with its business friendly regulatory environment, international experience, and global savoir-faire is able to introduce to global investors of the future a milieu of offshore products and asset protection vehicles in all capital markets.

Asset protection vehicles are not automatically offered in rich countries. Investors in rich countries will not automatically protect their assets, have higher income or enjoy the benefits of the same. Investors that thrive on these advantages may find that they are no longer the few taking pleasure from using legal ways to protect what they own, but are part of a global community of investors seeking the same benefits. The Harris Organisation has positioned itself to assist these investors and professionals to become beneficiaries of this trend.

Through its international network of offices and correspondents, The Harris Organisation is the Puente Del Mundo (Bridge of the World) for international commerce, finance, and management. The Harris Organisation can assist the investor by providing them with offshore financial services previously unavailable from poorly organized and overpriced traditional financial service providers.

In an era of man-made financial industries, the ratio of capital and labor becomes less important. Skills and knowledge, human capital, are created by the same investment funds that create physical capital. Today knowledge and skill now stand alone as the only source of comparative advantage in the global marketplace. That is why The Harris Organisation has organized over 150 of the sharpest minds in the world as its employees and hundreds of others as its correspondents. Those minds become available to the investors providing them with levels of expertise and international savoir-faire that even the world's largest financial firm's lack.

Offshore products have never been more important in global investing, although it is the application of these vehicles that counts. The Harris Organisation does not need to lead the world in the creation of new financial vehicles (even though we have), but rather perfect the application of these services to its traditional line of business. With our flexible size and agility, we are quite often the first to implement these products in the offshore marketplace. We have even taken that one step further by applying our products to the needs of independent investors. This ability further expands our position as a financial bridge to the rest of the world.

To be the masters in offering offshore products to global investors, The Harris Organisation manages a smooth flow from research, design, development, and communication to customer services that international competitors cannot match.

The secret of The Harris Organisation's success has been found, not in being either labor or capital intensive, or even in being management intensive, but in having the human capital base throughout our organisation that allows us to be the most efficient integrators of all of these offshore activities.

Prosperous offshore investing is not a birthright. In fact successful investors of the past not in tune with the global marketplace, may find themselves the losers in this new era. No investor acquires these skills without sacrifice and without making the investments necessary to create them. The Harris Organisation helps investors avoid the sacrifices necessary to compete in the new global offshore community.

Success or failure depends upon whether an investor is making a successful transition to the offshore industries of the future. The size of any particular investment is not important. The Harris Organisation allows the investor to maintain a comfortable size portfolio, but at the same time, provides them with asset protection services that even the largest financial firms are unable to provide.

If an individual wants to stay at the leading edge of investing so that they can continue to generate profits as well as protect their assets, they must be a participant in the evolutionary progress of the offshore industry so that they are in the right position to take advantage of the economic revolutions that arise. The Harris Organisation stays on top of this evolution for you, so you can focus on those things that matter most.

Forward thinking investors will not be left behind in this new era. In fact, The Harris Organisation can assist you in becoming the most agile offshore investor in this new economic world order with resulting benefits for you and your assets!

PART VIII
APPENDICES

APPENDIX A

(Model of Foundation Charter)

[NAME OF THE FOUNDATION]

FOUNDATION CHARTER

The undersigned [NAME OF THE FOUNDER], [sex], of age, [nationality], neighbor of this city, holder of personal identity document number [insert number here], with domicile in [physical domicile], Panama City, acting in the capacity of Founder, constitutes herewith in conformity with law No. 25 June 12, 1995, a Foundation of Private Interest with the following characteristics:

FIRST: *NAME.* The name of the Foundation is [NAME].

SECOND: *INITIAL FOUNDATION CAPITAL.* The initial foundation capital of the Foundation will be TEN THOUSAND DOLLARS, currency of legal tender in the United States of America. Sums of money or other properties may be incorporated on a regular basis, by the Founder, the Foundation Council or third persons. The transfer of property to the Foundation's patrimony may be carried out by public or private document. The Foundation's patrimony is exclusively reserved for the purposes mentioned in the present Foundation Charter and, therefore, the Foundation Council may not dispose of said patrimony in a manner different and contrary to what is established in the present Foundation Charter or in its regulations.

THIRD: *FOUNDATION COUNCIL.* The Foundation Council shall be composed by the following way:

President   [Name], personal identity document #. [number].
Secretary   [Name], personal identity document #. [number].
Treasury   [Name], personal identity document #. [number].

All with domicile in the Panama City, [physical domicile].

From the Regulations of the Foundation Council:

A. The Foundation Council is the supreme entity of the Foundation.

B. The Foundation Council may consist of natural and/or judicial persons.

C. The Founder initially appoints the Foundation Council. The election of the replacement of a member of the Foundation Council whether titleholder or alternate, by resignation, incapacity or demise, will require the votes of the simple majority of the remaining members of the Council. If there were no other members of the Foundation Council or if the remaining members are incapable, the Resident Agent of the Foundation shall be entitled to appoint the new members of the Foundation Council.

D. The office of the members of the Council is for an indefinite period of time.

E. The Foundation Council is responsible for the management and representation of the Foundation, in an unlimited manner, before third persons, especially before the foreign or national judicial and governmental authorities.

F. The Foundation Council is entitled to delegate to one or several of its members, or to a third person, its power regarding the issuance of the Foundation's regulations, as well as to assign its responsibility for the administration and representation of the Foundation, for specific affairs, in which case, it will bestow the Foundation with the right to sign and bind.

G. The members of the Foundation Council are authorized to exercise signatory powers on behalf of the Foundation and will not be obliged to respond to third parties as to their competence to give instructions and make arrangements, however, they will always act within the authority of a valid resolution of the Foundation Council. The right and the form of signature to bind the Foundation may be established initially by the Founder. Subsequently, the Foundation Council will have said authority.

H. If the Foundation Council is comprised of more than one member, it shall constitute itself and will elect one President, a Secretary and any other officer. The Foundation Council's resolutions will be valid if all the members are duly summoned and if the majority of them are present. The resolution of the Foundation Council will be passed with simple majority of the members present. In the event of parity, the President will have the deciding vote.

I. Should the Foundation Council be comprised of two members, its resolutions will require a unanimous decision.

J. Should the Foundation Council be comprised of only one member such member alone shall make the decisions and pass resolutions. Said resolutions shall be signed by a person appointed by the Board of Directors of this sole member.

K. Resolutions of the Foundation Council shall be recorded in Minutes and the Secretary, who will keep the minutes, will sign these.

L. The Foundation Council shall meet by invitation of the President at the domicile of the Foundation, or at such other place as may be designated by the Foundation Council.

M. The resolutions of the Foundation Council may also be taken by means of a circular letter in which case a unanimous vote will be required.

N. The Foundation Council its obligation is always is of middle safe pact in contrary or guarantee clause.

FOURTH: *DOMICILE.* The domicile of the Foundation is in the Republic of Panama. By resolution of the Foundation Council, the domicile of the Foundation may be transferred, at any time, to another place in Panama or in a foreign country. All the legal relationships arising from the constitution and existence of the Foundation will be subject to the law in force at the domicile of the Foundation. The competent courts of jurisdiction for the foundation are the ones of its domicile. In the event of the Foundation's domicile being transferred, the provisions of the law on Foundations of Private Interest of the Republic of Panama shall remain applicable to the foundation insofar as compelling provisions at the foundation's new domicile do not demand otherwise.

FIFTH: *RESIDENT AGENT.* The resident agent of the Foundation is the law firm Lineros, Hidalgo y Asociados, located in Avenida Balboa, Edificio Balboa Plaza, Second floor, Office # 210, Panama City, Republic of Panama.

SIXTH: *PURPOSE.* The purpose of the Foundation is to conserve the assets and to carry out the administration and management of the assigned patrimony based on the rules and terms if they should exist. It may also pay for the education, living expenses, preparation and assistance, as well as the general maintenance costs, or other similar help, of one or several members of the families determined in the charter. In addition to the members of one or several families, the Foundation may benefit other natural or judicial persons or institutions of any nature and take the necessary provisions for the orderly succession of its patrimony. To attain its purposes, the Foundation must properly preserve, administrate and invest its patrimony. The Foundation must not pursue profit purposes; nevertheless, it may carry out commercial activities in a non -customary manner, or exercise the rights which proceed from the representative titles of the commercial companies that form the Foundation's patrimony, as long as the economic result or product of said activities is exclusively dedicated to the purposes of this Foundation. It may also devote itself to any other licit activity permitted by these types of entities, as may be determined by the Founder or the Foundation Council.

SEVENTH: *BENEFICIARIES.*

1. The Founder, at the time of creating the Foundation, or subsequently the Foundation Council, may create a private document known as the regulations whereby the beneficiaries will be designated and everything else that relates to them will be determined. The Foundation Council will distribute the patrimony and the Foundation's revenue, in full or in part, to one or several beneficiaries in accordance with the provisions of the regulations

2. Distributions to the designated beneficiary or beneficiaries, as well as the timing and extent of said distribution, will be subject to the dispositions established in the regulations.

3. It is expressly stipulated that the beneficiaries are neither the Foundation's owners or creditors, therefore, they may not with validity bring any claim before the Foundation other than those founded in the terms of the Foundations Charter, the regulations and/or resolutions passed by the Foundation Council.

EIGHTH: *AMENDMENTS TO THE FOUNDATION CHART.* The Founder and the Foundation Council (by unanimous consent) may amend the present Foundation Statutes. The Founder and the Foundation Council may amend, remove or declare inapplicable one or more dispositions of the present Foundation statutes, change or eliminate all or any of the beneficiaries, name or add new beneficiaries, increase, decrease or in any other manner amend the benefits of all and any of the beneficiaries, add new assets to the foundation's patrimony and amend the Foundation's statutes in any other manner.

NINTH: *DURATION*. The period of duration of the Foundation will not be limited and may only be dissolved by unanimous decision of the Foundation Council or the Founder or based on the causes foreseen by the law for the termination of the Foundation.

TENTH: *DISTRIBUTION OF THE BENEFITS*. The Foundation Council may distribute the capital or interests of this Foundation in accordance with what is established in the statutes, which will be amended at any time by the Founder or the Foundation Council.

ELEVENTH: *ANNUAL ACCOUNT*. The Foundation Council should render account of its actions annually to:

1. The Founder, until his demise.

2. The beneficiaries or beneficiaries, on the death of the Founder.

3. The Protector if there is one.

If there should not be any objections within ninety (90) days, counted, as of the date in which it was received, it will be considered approved. Once this period of time has passed or the account approved, the members of the Foundation Council will be exonerated from their responsibility for their action, but said approval does not exonerate them before the beneficiaries or third persons who should have an interest in the Foundation, for the damages caused by serious guilt or fraud in the Foundation's administration.

TWELFTH: *REMOVAL OF THE FOUNDATION COUNCIL*. The Foundation Council may be removed by the Founder or by the Protector, if any. At the same time, the Founder or Protector may appoint or add new members to the Foundation Council.

THIRTEENTH: *OBLIGATIONS AND DUTIES OF THE FOUNDATION COUNCIL*. The Foundation Council will have the following obligations and duties:

(a) To administer the Foundation's assets in accordance with the present Foundation statutes or its charter.

To carry out acts, contracts or lawful businesses which are convenient, adequate or necessary to fulfill the Foundation's purposes and to include in such contract, agreements and other instruments and obligations, such clauses and conditions as are necessary or convenient, and which are in accordance with that the purposes of the Foundation and which are not contrary to the law, morale, good customs and public order.

a) To inform the beneficiaries of the Foundation of its economic situation, in accordance with what is established in the Foundation statutes and its charter.

b) To deliver the beneficiaries of the Foundation the property and resources that have been designated in their favor in the Foundation Charter or its regulations.

c) To carry out all such actions or contracts permitted to the Foundation, in accordance with Law 25 of 12 June 1995, and any other legal or regulatory dispositions that may be applicable.

FOURTEENTH: *PROTECTOR-PROFESSIONAL ADVISOR-AUDITOR.* The Foundation Council may appoint a supervisory entity which may be natural or judicial persons, which may be called Protector, Professional Advisor, Auditor or any similar name and which may exercise any of the following powers:

a) To ensure the compliance of the purposes of the Foundation on the part of the Foundation Council and to safeguard the rights and interests of the beneficiaries.

b) To require the Foundation Council to render accounts.

c) To modify the purposes and objectives of the Foundation, when compliance is impossible or of difficult performance.

d) To appoint new members of the Foundation Council by reason of temporary, permanent or accidental absence, or due to the expiration of the period for which they were appointed.

e) To appoint new members in replacement of existing members in the event of temporary or accidental absence, add or reduce the number of members of the Foundation Council.

f) To approve the acts adopted by the Foundation Council, pursuant to the Foundation Charter or its regulations.

g) To supervise the management of the Foundation's assets and to control their application to the purposes and objectives established in the Foundation Charter.

h) To exclude the Foundation's Beneficiaries and add others, in accordance to what is determined in the Foundation Charter or it statues.

FIFTEENTH: *LIQUIDATION AND DISSOLUTION.*

A. The Foundation Council is authorized to dissolve the Foundation and to appoint one or more liquidators if it shall be necessary.

B. In the event of dissolution and after payment of any and all debts and obligations, the liquidation shall proceed according to the provisions in favor of the beneficiaries established in the regulations. In case there are no beneficiaries, the Foundation Council shall resolve the final destination of assets of the Foundation. The resolution of dissolution issued by the Foundation Council shall be duly registered in the Public Register of the Republic of Panama.

The Foundation may also be dissolved due to the following reasons:

a) Due to non-fulfillment of the purposes for which it was formed or because its fulfillment becomes impossible.

b) If it becomes insolvent, incapable of making payments or because of bankruptcy proceedings.

c) Due to the loss or total extinction of the assets of the Foundation.

SIXTEENTH: *REGULATIONS.* The Founder and the Foundation Council are authorized to issue the Foundation regulations, at the time of creating the Foundation or subsequently. The same will be included:

1. The manner in which the Foundation's patrimony will be administrated.

2. The Foundation's beneficiaries.

3. The manner in which the beneficiaries should be excluded or added.

4. The benefits that shall correspond to the Beneficiaries.

5. The manner in which the Foundation Council will advise the beneficiaries of the Foundation patrimony.

6. The manner in which the assets and products that have been established in their favor will be liquidated.

7. The powers of the Foundation Council specific or complementary for the fulfillment of its purposes.

8. The appointment of the Protector and any other supervisory entity.

9. The manner in which the liquidation of the Foundation's patrimony will be carried out in the case of the Foundation's dissolution.

SEVENTEENTH: *ANNOUNCEMENTS.* The announcements required by law or by the regulations shall be made in any daily Panamanian newspaper of ample circulation.

EIGHTEENTH: *LEGAL REPRESENTATIVE.* If the Foundation Council is made up of more than one member, the Legal Representative will be the President, in his absence the Secretary or the natural or judicial person that the Foundation Council should appoint for this purpose. If the Foundation Council is made up of one member, that member will be the Legal Representative. The Legal Representative will be appointed and removed by the Foundation Council.

NINETEENTH: *RIGHT OF SIGNATURE BEFORE THIRD PERSONS.* The signature of the Foundation's Legal Representative when the Foundation Council is formed by one judicial person or the joint signatures of any two members of the Foundation Council, when it is formed by more than one person, in respect to any act, transaction or business of the Foundation, shall be binding on the same, without prejudice of the formalities described in the Third Article of the present Foundation Chart.

TWENTIETH: *ARBITRATION.* Any type of conflict arising from or related to the Foundation, this Foundation Chart or its Regulations, as well as the interpretation, application, execution and termination of the same, must be resolved by arbitration, in accordance with the regulations of the Center of Conciliation and Arbitration of the Panamanian Chamber of Commerce, Industry and Agriculture.

TWENTY-FIRST: CHANGE *OF JURISDICTION.* When the Foundation Council or the Protector, if there is any, at their sole and absolute discretion consider it necessary, they can transfer the foundation to the jurisdiction of another country complying with the requirements foreseen by the law.

TWENTY SECOND: LIQUIDATION. In the case of liquidation the property is returned to the Founder's patrimony, failing which, to the legal or natural person named by the regulations.

TWENTY-THIRD: SEAL. The Foundation can, if it so deems convenient, have its own seal.

APPENDIX B

MODEL OF REGULATION OF THE FOUNDATION

FOUNDATION NAME

FOUNDATION BYLAWS

The Foundation Council, administrative entity by virtue of article 17 of Law 25 of June 12 1995, develops this **BYLAWS**, that is in accordance with the objects of the Memorandum of the Foundation of the Foundation of Private Interest named _____ and duly registered at Filing Card _____, Roll _____, Image _____, of the Private Interest Foundation Section of the Public Registry that is developed under the following terms:

I. RULES OF INTERPRETATION

The Bylaws must be interpreted at all times in agreement with the objects of the Memorandum of the Foundation or in lack of it, by virtue of the spirit and desire of the Founder.

II. POWERS OF THE FOUNDER

The Founder may designate one or more beneficiaries at any time. The beneficiaries may be determined in separate documents. The Founder can revoke the beneficiary(ies) in a unilateral manner before maturity date or compliance with the condition, as long as the effects have been complied with or caused.

III. THE CHARTER OF THE BENEFICIARY

The rights of the beneficiary(ies) shall be contingent to what it is indicated in the Law, or, to the objects of the Foundation of Private Interest by the Founder. The beneficiary(ies) can receive the benefits or utilities of the assets according to the instructions or turn of activity of the Foundation, through a clause or express designation, so stipulated.

The right of the beneficiary(ies) depends on the formality by which the Foundation was created.

IV. ADMINISTRATION AND INVESTMENT OF THE FOUNDATION FUNDS

The Administration Council can administer the possessions and assets transferred in the Memorandum of the Foundation or subsequent to the registration of the Memorandum of the Foundation.

The Administration of the funds and investments shall be subject to the regulations related to due diligence established in the Law and based on the good businessman's rules and in good faith.

The Founder can designate an administrator or guardian to deliver the Founder's instructions.

The Foundation Council can impart instructions or dispose of the assets and guarantee them though the approval of the Founder or whomever s/he designates.

The Foundation Council or the Agent, or, that person that intervenes for the beneficiary(ies) for the management or administration of the possessions can retain a commission for rendering his/her services according to the rules and practices of the market.

The Foundation Council can handle transactions only with the purpose of guarantying the protection of the assets given to the Foundation.

V. LIQUIDATION OF THE FOUNDATION

The liquidation shall comply with similar rules applicable to corporations, unless a special process is applicable at that moment.

The annex as well as any eventual amendment binds the Foundation Council and the corresponding entities.

The Founder declares to know the Bylaws of the Foundation hereby extended, in witness thereof she signs it as an indication of her conformity with its content.

_____

FOUNDER

Designation of the Beneficiaries

I, _____, as Founder of the Foundation of Private Interest named _____, which is duly registered in the Public Registry at Filing Card _____, Roll _____, Image _____, whose Registered Agent is the law firm **Lineros, Hidalgo y Asociados**, hereby appoint as beneficiaries of the Foundation:

1.
2.
3.

HIERARCHY OF THE BENEFICIARIES:

It is designated as beneficiaries in case of death or upon completion of the condition the following persons whose hierarchy of beneficiary shall be in the following order:

1.
2.
3.
4.

STATUTE OF THE BENEFICIARIES

In case of underage beneficiaries, the Foundation Council or the designated person shall distribute the funds in equal parts except instructions to the contrary.

In case of beneficiaries without a tutor, curator or protector, the Foundation Council shall administer with the diligence of a reasonable man the assets given to the Foundation.

In the City of Panama, on the _____ day of the month of _____ of _____.

_____

FOUNDER

APPENDIX C

Model of Foundation Resolution

[NAME OF THE FOUNDATION

FOUNDATION RESOLUTION

The Foundation Council, acting in accordance with the authority granted in the Third Clause of the Foundation Charter, properly called a meeting which was held in [place], on [date], in order to grant General Power of Administration and Management to [NAME], bearing Identity Document   , domiciled at [physical domicile], whose profession is [profession], so that he/she may dispose, administer and manage the property or capital of this Foundation either within the Republic of Panama or abroad, in the local or international markets according to his/her best knowledge. Furthermore he/she shall be entitled to conduct any kind of transactions on real or personal property, securities, participation interests, expert witnesses or lawyers, create corporations, submit any tax or financial planning, affect, encumber, mortgage property, set up trusts, antichresis and establish all the investment machinery for the benefit of the Foundation, directing the above-described activity to the Foundation purpose, for which said Foundation has been created.

Granted in the City of Panama, on the _____day of the month of _____ of _____.

_____   _____
[NAME]   [NAME]
President   Secretary

APPENDIX D

RELEVANT ADVANTAGES FOR FOREIGN INVESTORS IN PANAMA

◆ A democratic government that firmly believes in the concept of private enterprise and that encourages foreign investment.

◆ A privileged and strategic location that highly facilitates world communications, transportation and trade commerce in general.

◆ Foreigners and Panamanians are viewed as equals under the Constitution.

◆ An international banking center that operates freely in all currencies and creates a financial climate that encourages the free movement of funds.

◆ No taxes on interest earned on time and savings deposits.

◆ Unique monetary system based on the US dollar with no restrictions on monetary transfers to and from the country or on the conversion and circulation of the US dollar.

◆ No central bank or money issuing authority.

◆ An economy that is virtually inflation free which makes the cost of living in Panama generally lower than any European or North and South American cities.

◆ A tax law anchored on the principle of territoriality that does not consider as taxable income revenues originating from transactions that take place outside Panama (offshore) even when they are managed from within Panama.

◆ A corporation law which is very flexible about the purpose of a corporation, amount of capital, the nationality of shareholders, bearer shares, and the geographic scope of operations.

◆ No restrictions on corporate mergers or acquisitions.

◆ A flexible maritime law coupled with an international maritime center for ship repair and supply of water, foodstuffs, maritime equipment and fuel for ships using the Panama Canal and the ports of Balboa and Cristobal.

◆ Colon Free Zone, the first and largest in the Western Hemisphere, and one of the most successful in the word.

◆ Incentives for industrial, agroindustrial and touristic investments.

APPENDIX E

TAX EXEMPTS IN PANAMA

FOREIGN SOURCES

1. Income from real estate located abroad or from personal property outside of Panama, regardless of whether the owner of such property resides in Panama or administers the property from Panama;

2. Income derived from the practice of a profession or the rendering of services outside of Panama;

3. Interests earned on loans used by the debtor outside of the country, even though the loan agreement was formalized in Panama and the creditor carries on business in Panama;

4. Profits from the sale of goods not entering the territory of Panama, even though the invoicing takes place from an office in Panama;

5. Income derived from an agreement executed in Panama, even though the agreement is carried out or perfected abroad;

6. Income derived from insurance business, provided that the risk insured covers property or persons located or domiciled abroad, regardless of whether the agreement was executed in Panama or business activities of the insurer are carried out in Panama;

7. Income from industrial property rights (patents, trademarks, utility models, etc.), provided that such patents, trademarks, and models are used outside of Panama; and

8. Dividends paid by a Panamanian company with its principal place of business in Panama, where the business income is generated from foreign sources, or from certain kinds of income from Panamanian sources that are tax-exempt.

PANAMANIAN SOURCES

1. Interest on bank deposits in banks established in Panama;

2. Interest earned on loans granted to finance the construction of low-cost housing projects in Panama;

3. Interest earned on loans granted to finance certain agricultural activities in Panama, provided that the yearly interest rates does not exceed 8%;

4. Interest earned on loans granted or bonds issued by the Panamanian Government;

5. Interest on loans granted to finance the development of tourism and reforestation in Panama;

6. Interest paid to certain institutions, international organizations and foreign governments;

7. Income from the commercialization of Panamanian forest products;

8. Income from international maritime transportation carried out on vessels bearing the Panamanian flag, even if the charter agreements are entered into in Panama; and

9. Royalties paid to persons domiciled abroad by companies established in the Colon Free Zone.

PART IX

ABOUT THE AUTHOR

About the Author

Marc M. Harris graduated from North Carolina Wesleyan College with a 4.0 average at the age of 18. Shortly thereafter, while still only 18, he passed his Certified Public Accountant (CPA) examination and is believed to be the youngest person in the United States to accomplish this. He went on to Columbia University for his MBA with a concentration in Investment Finance.

After completing his formal education, Mr. Harris set out to apply himself in the business world. He found it difficult to secure a professional position because of his age and when he finally did, he found himself unable to realize his full potential. On December 2, 1985, with little more than pocket change, young Mr. Harris started his own company.

After substantial changes in the American tax law in 1986, Mr. Harris refocussed the firm's strategy in favor of international tax planning and legitimate methods for Americans to take advantage of offshore tax havens. In order to better service his growing international clientele, he relocated the center of operations to Panama. Today, with over 150 employees, The Firm of Marc M. Harris, Inc. has become the largest independent provider of quality international financial services in Latin America and the Caribbean.

Mr. Harris has not only built his company, but has personally received many awards which include the key to the city of Miami Beach and Most Distinguished Alumni at North Carolina Wesleyan College. He has established a personal foundation that contributes to Panamanian society by funding nutritional projects and helping needy families in the community. He is a much sought-after speaker on international financial planning and gives seminars throughout the world. Mr. Harris has assisted in drafting new financial services legislation for several Latin American countries and is a contributor to various financial journals and newsletters on a regular basis.

The Firm of Marc M. Harris, Inc. opens a whole new world of business and financial opportunities for its clients. We can improve your financial profile and make you a world-class investor.

The Harris Organisation is a diversified financial services institution providing individual and corporate clients with a broad range of international structures in the financial and asset protection areas and investment opportunities throughout the world.

ABOUT THE AUTHOR

As a full-service provider of international financial planning, we offer our clients the following specialized services:

- The creation and administration of legal and fiduciary structures designed to best serve the client's personal and/or business requirements.

- Detailed tax, estate, financial and business planning.

- Special analysis of commercial situations for opportunity enhancement.

- The total administration of all entities under our responsibility to include compliance with all legal requirements as needed for pertinent jurisdictions.

- The preparation of all domestic and foreign documents, income tax returns and nominee services as required.

- Complete international investment services through our own full-service discount brokerage department.

- Access to the Firm's broad range of securities and investment opportunities unavailable through other channels.

For more information, please write to:

The Harris Organisation
Attn: Traditional Client Services
Apartado Postal 0832-0835
World Trade Center
Panama, Republic of Panama
Or fax +507 263-6964, marking your fax "Attn: Traditional Client Services."

THE PRIVATE INTEREST FOUNDATION OF PANAMA

You may also contact us by e-mail at

globalinvesting@marc-harris.com

Initial contact by telephone is not recommended, so that your question may be directed to the person on the staff best able to handle it. The more information you can provide about your needs on your initial inquiry will make it easier to give you precisely the information you need.

LaVergne, TN USA
02 January 2010
210710LV00009B/252/A